NEW ARCHITECTURE
The New Moderns & The Super Moderns

Claudio Silvestrin, Dairy Factory transformed into offices for a book dealer & art collector, London 1987. see pp90-93

NALBACK, SCHEME FOR PARIS, MONUMENT OR MODEL OF THOUGHT

An Architectural Design Profile

NEW ARCHITECTURE
The New Moderns & The Super Moderns

NORMAN FOSTER, KING'S CROSS MASTER PLAN

ACADEMY EDITIONS

Acknowledgements: All illustrations supplied by the architects unless otherwise stated.

Charles Jencks, The New Moderns pp6-18 is an extract from his forthcoming book of the same title to be published by Academy Editions; p10 & Half Title Frank O'Gehry, Vitra Museum, West Germany, illustration supplied by Vitra Ltd, London & Vitra International, Basel; p12 Peter Eisenman, The Wexner Centre, illustration from *AD* 11/12 89. All other illlustrations are taken from the book.

Kenneth Frampton, Rappel à l'ordre, the Case for the Tectonic pp19-27, is broadly based on a lecture given at the first international cubit symposium on Constancy and Change in Architecture held at Texas A&M University. We are grateful to the university authorities, symposium organisers and Malcolm Quantrill for permission to reproduce it here. There are further plans to publish the papers given at the Symposium in the first issue of the Cubit Review in January 1991. Illustrations supplied by the author.

Conrad Jameson, The Super Moderns pp26-33; p28 is a pre-publication extract from the book of the same title, computer image of Barcelona Pavilion by Andrew Adams, first published in *A&D*, 2-86, painting taken from *Braque* by Serge Fauchereau published by Academy Editions; p30 Pantheon photo taken by Charles Jencks; p31 Essex University, photo provided by the University.

Rob Krier, Gustav Peichl, pp34-35 was written on the occasion of an exhibition of Gustav Peichl's work at the RIBA; reproduced with the kind permission of the author.

Norman Foster, Kings Cross Master Plan pp36-43, is an edited version of the lecture first given at the RIBA.

Rolling Stones, Steel Wheels Tour pp44-61. We are grateful to Mark Fisher for his assistance and also to Mark Norton of 41 Collaboration for his work in designing the article. We would also like to thank Lynne Tanzman of The Rolling Stones public relations department for arranging the interview between Mick Jagger and Andreas Papadakis.

Daniel Libeskind, The Jewish Extension to the Berlin Museum pp62-77. Collaborators: Marina Stankovic, Donald Bates, Attilio Terragni, Marco Vido, with the assistance of Jyrki Sinkkila, Edwin Engler, Ernst Struwig, Shinn Tadakoro. Consultant: Dr Kurt Forster

Berlin/Paris, Monuments or Models of Thought, pp78-89, this feature was prepared with the cooperation of Kristin Feireiss, organiser and editor of the following two publications both published by Ernst and Sohn, Berlin. *Berlin - Denkmal oder Denkmodell? Architektonische Entwurfe fur den Aufbruch in das 21 Jahrhunder* catalogue and forthcoming *Paris, Architecture and Utopia*.

We wish to thank Will Alsop for his assistance.

Claudio Silvestrin, Recent Projects pp90-93, Photographs by Alberto Piovano, Ian Dobby and the architect.

EDITOR
Dr Andreas Papadakis
EDITORIAL OFFICES: 42 LEINSTER GARDENS, LONDON W2 3AN TELEPHONE: 071-402 2141
HOUSE EDITOR: Maggie Toy DESIGNED BY: Andrea Bettella, Mario Bettella SUBSCRIPTIONS MANAGER: Mira Joka
CONSULTANTS: Catherine Cooke, Dennis Crompton, Terry Farrell, Kenneth Frampton, Charles Jencks, Henrich Koltz, Leon Krier, Robert
Maxwell, Demetri Porphyrios, Colin Rowe, Derek Walker

Republished in great Britain in 1993 by Architectural Design
an imprint of the
ACADEMY GROUP LTD
MEMBER OF THE VCH PUBLISHING GROUP
42 LEINSTER GARDENS, LONDON W2 3AN
First published in 1990

ISBN: 1 85490 201 6

Distributed in the United States of America by
ST MARTINS PRESS, 175 FIFTH AVENUE, NEW YORK 100010

Printed and bound in Singapore

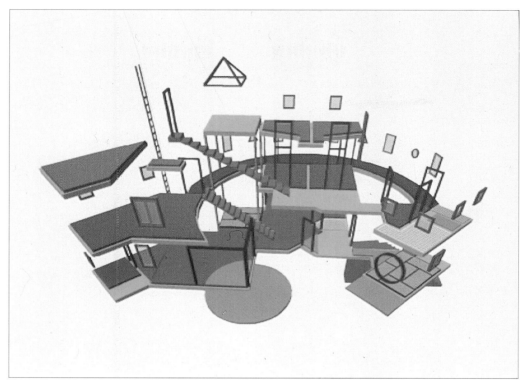

HISASHI HARA, NA N JA MO N JA, DISSECTED PERSPECTIVE

Contents

OMA, ZKM CENTRE FOR ART AND MEDIA TECHNOLOGY, KARLSRUHE, WEST GERMANY

CHARLES JENCKS
THE NEW MODERNS

ITSUKO HASEGAWA, BIZAN HALL, SHIZUOKO, JAPAN

The following article is reproduced here to coincide with the publication of the author's latest book
'The New Moderns' in which he argues that Modernism has reappeared in a new form. As in previous
revivals it enjoys nothing so much as dying in order to be reborn. Modernism according to this theory
is the style of the bourgeoisie and is based on continual destruction-construction cycles.

'Nothing is so dangerous as being too modern, one is apt to grow old-fashioned quite suddenly.'   Oscar Wilde

Nothing will more effectively reinvigorate Modernism than killing it off. Like a voracious phoenix Modernism not only rises from its ashes but positively feeds off them. It has died many times since its mythical 1820s birth with the notion of the avant-garde in France. A particularly fertile period of Modernism in Europe, from 1870 to 1900, led to such boredom with the 'old-fashioned new' that it was declared dead in Samuel Lublinski's *Der Ausgang der Moderne* (*The Exit of the Modern*, Dresden 1909). But then the next year Virginia Woolf saw it rise anew: 'On or about December 1910 human nature changed . . . All human relations shifted – those between masters and servants, husbands and wives, parents and children. And when human relations change there is at the same time a change in religion, conduct, politics and literature'.

1910, the year of the first Post-Impressionist Exhibition and the death of King Edward VII, was an *annus mirabilis* for Modernism in literature and the arts, but for architecture the end of the First World War marks the re-rise of the movements, when all competing 'isms' claimed the birth of a new era: Purism, Dadaism, Expressionism, Constructivism, Neo-Plasticism – to name but a few of the contenders for the new New.

There's nothing like the end of a world war to signal a shift in culture and establish a conceptual *tabula rasa*. *L'Esprit Nouveau*, Le Corbusier and Ozenfant's journal, summarised some of this born-again 'new spirit' – a phrase that already had quite a venerable history in the nineteenth century. Fiercely polemical, this new *Zeitgeist* was set in opposition to academicism and the reigning Ecole des Beaux-Arts , reminding us (after the idea of its murder/rebirth) of the second great truth of Modernism: not only must it feed off the corpse of its predecessor and thrive on the *tabula rasa*, but it must be against the reigning culture – the *arrière-garde*, whether this is real or fictitious. To be new Modernism must characterise any opposition as staid, nostalgic and uncreative, or else it fails to re-establish credentials as the avant-garde. From this it follows as night the day that Modernism and (for want of a better word) Traditionalism have a vested interest in keeping each other in place. For logical and political reasons, the health of the former depends on the existence of the latter.

What about the 'New Moderns' today? This slightly ridiculous and certainly redundant label once again proves the truths of our little theorem. It has probably popped up in all the arts as a reaction against a renewed traditionalism. And in architecture it has emerged fully born from the ruins of the International Style (and cognate modes) and in opposition to what it now characterises as old-hat: Post-Modernism. In fact this last movement almost deserves the credit for galvanising the New Mods into action: like a loathed political party which has been in power too long it has helped crystallise a unified opposition.

The birth of the New Mods (and a phoenix should always have a precise moment of ascension) was in Spring 1977 when Peter Eisenman published his editorial 'Post-Functionalism', in the pages of his significantly named magazine *Oppositions*. Reacting to two exhibitions *Architettura Razionale*,1973, and 'Ecole des Beaux-Arts', at the Museum of Modern Art (a Vatican of the New),1975, Eisenman characterised both exhibitions as Post-Modern and, what was even worse, well within the five hundred year-old tradition of humanism. To this decrepit dinosaur he opposed, inevitable, a Modernism that was anti-humanist. Basically it summarised the currents of 19th- and 20th-century art that were abstract, atonal and atemporal. The tactic of being a-anything was as typical as being non- or dis- other things. Modernism proceeds by negations, like the phoenix.

Using Michel Foucault's idea of a new *épistémè* which breaks with humanism, Eisenman postulates a new modern architecture that displaces 'man away from the centre of his world', negates

Modernism, and it appears in a *Newsweek* article by Douglas Davis to describe a new mood and style: 'Elegant New Geometry'. Davis gives several key examples of the kind of architecture I had termed Late-Modern: the Hong Kong Bank, Richard Rogers' Inmos Factory, a Gwathmey-Siegel house and their revivals of Modern furniture – the Neo-Hoffman and Neo-Mackintosh chairs on which Meier and others were ringing the changes. Were these really 'Neo' or rather really 'Late'? – and does it matter?

For a movement to be adequately 'neo' there must be a sufficient period of death, mourning and reconsideration before a revival. After all the phoenix waits five or six centuries in the desert before arising and Neo-Classicism – the model for all true 'Neo's' – waited fifteen centuries before reviving Roman dress and other customs. Without a sufficient period for both forgetting and reconsidering the past, one has 'survivals' not 'revivals'. This is one reason I would dispute Davis' hasty application of the term to Norman Foster, Richard Rogers and a host of other architects. They consider themselves a *continuation* not a re-invention of Modernism. But he and those critics, such as Paul Goldberger, who started using 'neo-modern' would argue that

L TO *R*: TOYO ITO, SILVER HUT; RICHARD MEIER, MUSEUM FOR THE DECORATIVE ARTS, FRANKFURT

the idea of authorship and functionalism and puts in their place an 'atemporal, decompositional mode', a method of design with form 'understood as a series of fragments – signs without meaning'. If this sounds familiar it's because Deconstruction had already by then invaded the most prestigious departments of literature in the Ivy League, and has now become an orthodoxy. As often happens, a literary event preceded an architectural one: the written and spoken word led a change in the more dependent sign systems, the visual arts and architecture.

The phrase 'neo-modern' started to be mentioned in New York circles about 1982 and it's probably no accident that the *Zeitgeist* picked this city to re-launch its hardy bird. Here the debate with Post-Modernists was most acute, while Johnson's AT&T building had just been finished – a monumental classical slab which seemed to represent nothing so much as the gravestone of Modernism and a change of heart for one of its former protagonists.

I can't remember where I first heard or read the term 'neo-modern', but I believe it was Ada Louise Huxtable referring to the work of Richard Meier. In any case by 1983 many New York critics had started to adopt it as a polemical counterpoint to Post-

although there is an unbroken continuity of the Modern tradition, there is also a fundamental change in attitude.

The New-Moderns they say are no longer utopians who wish to change society but rather aesthetes who play with Modernist forms: their essential message is not ethical but stylistic, a new baroque elaboration of the language synthesised in the twenties. Goldberger claims that the ultimate neo-modern buildings are Bernard Tschumi's *folies* at the Parc de la Villette because they are Mannerist fantasies with no social or ideological intentions. This assertion is both right and wrong: right because Tschumi's fire-engin red pavilions are an elaborate play with Constructivist forms arising from Chernikhov, and wrong because Mannerism is also characteristic of Late- and Post-Modern architecture, and Tschumi intends these *folies* to illustrate the theories of Deconstruction.

It is this ideology, akin to Eisenman's, which really defines the New Modernism: it is indeed new to architecture. Anti-humanism, decentring, the 'displacement of man away from the centre of his world', in Eisenman's words, may have existed in Modern literature and philosophy, but these disruptions did not happen in architecture. The reason is obvious. Architects, until recently, had to justify their buildings functionally and positively as furthering the goals of society. Now the New Moderns no longer believe in this humanism; rather they present their work as a self-justifying play with metaphysical ideas. The key architects who follow this agenda are Eisenman, Tschumi, Libeskind, Fujii, Gehry, Koolhaas, Hadid, Morphosis and Hejduk, but not Foster, Rogers, Hopkins, Maki and Pei. The former are Neo-Modernists and Deconstructionists, the latter are Late-Modernists who continue the Modern Movement in an elaborate and complex form.

The Power and Weakness of Labels

But do these distinctions matter? There are some architects, such as Richard Meier, who consider themselves neo-modern and use the term polemically as a stick to beat Post-Modernists. There are others, such as Coop Himmelblau, Philip Johnson and Peter Cook, who might find themselves cutting back and forth between all styles and ideologies. And most architects, likr most people, are bored by labels, finding them reductive and constricting, like ill-fitting suits.

There is much to be said for the view that all labels – stylistic,

ing both the suspension and re-fashioning of concepts – so too does the experience of architecture. Hence when we confront a new development, or marginal variation of tradition, we must invent a new terminology that catches these nuances.

In the last twenty years of writing on architecture I have developed a dense thicket of terms and their branching relations which together become 'evolutionary trees' – undulating and pulsating diagrams which show the dynamic development of schools, ideas and architects. The basis for this classification is admittedly eclectic, partly the result of following structuralist theories of Claude Lévi-Strauss, and ordinary evolutionary diagrams familiar in biology. Also I have made use of George Kubler's idea of 'fibrous bundles' developed in his book *The Shape of Time*,[7] and the idea of Anthony Blunt that any movement consists of many definers, many more than the usual four or five given in textbooks on art. Finally, my undulating diagrams, with their many terms, come from the observation that architecture today is characterised by fragmentation, pluralism and mutual opposition. All of this has led to my classification of current architecture into two basic traditions: Late- and Post-Modernism. This classification has its discontents but it has been

NORMAN FOSTER, STOCKLEY PARK

ideological, historical – distort the perception of architecture and reduce it to verbal categories. This contamination by language cannot be denied: architecture is created and perceived through non-linguistic codes which have their own integrity, and words can just get in the way. At the same time, however, words and classifications cannot be avoided in creation and perception. As semiologists have shown, our universe is fatally immersed in the linguistic sign, the most dominant sign system of all. It follows that the only escape from a bad label is a better one; or rather a complex set of classifiers which does justice to the rich diversity of intentions in a building.

E H Gombrich has shown the ambivalence of all labels in his essay 'Norm and Form' which includes a section labelled very poignantly 'Classification and its Discontents'. There is no lover of art, he says, who is not impatient with the academic historian and his concern with pigeonholes. Any work of art is unique, ineffable and demands a fresh experience on its own terms – a suspension of disbelief and the habitual categories of classification. And yet, as he also points out, any experience of art is made through concepts which also have their own pre-existence and autonomy. If all art perception has this double aspect – demand-

partially accepted by many historians and architects.

The most controversial aspects of this division, I suppose, are the relative value given to Post-Modernism and the question of whether Late-Modernists aren't really just 'Modernists' as many architects still call themselves. I have argued at length that they differ in style and intention from the 'High Modernists' – Le Corbusier, Gropius, Mies and others who established the paradigm in the twenties – and so demand another prefix to mark this distinction, but I can understand their reluctance to use such an unwieldly and slightly negative term as 'Late'; it sounds like they are at the end of a dying tradition. My belief is that indeed the paradigm is ending, but it will probably go on – as did Late-Gothic, Late-Renaissance and Late-Baroque – for another hundred years. In the final analysis Modernism is the ideology and style of modernisation and both will last until the Second and Third Worlds are fully industralised and the problems of modernisation are so acute everywhere that a Post-Modern paradigm is adopted by the whole world. At that point ecology and semiology, not economy and materialism, will be the leading modes of thought – obviously not something that is going to happen tomorrow.

ABOVE: FRANK GEHRY, THE VITRA DESIGN MUSEUM, WEIL AM RHEIN, WEST GERMANY

Thus 'Late-Modern' can be a relatively neutral descriptive term which has a positive future. Indeed Late-Modern architects often now out-perform their traditional and Post-Modern competitors, just as the cross-bow out-performed the rifle for fifty years, when it was threatened by obsolescence. The challenge of Post-Modernism, I would argue, has made both Neo- and Late-Modernism flourish, an ironic situation for all concerned. Indeed when I came to write on architecture of the 1980s, in *Architecture Today*, I devoted almost twice as much space to Late- as to Post-Modern developments – not obviously because I prefer this tradition, but rather because it has been more productive and in some senses more 'creative'.

In any case the point I want to stress is that these terms are relational and refer to a network of classifiers. As Anthony Blunt points out in *Some Uses and Misuses of the terms Baroque and Rococo as applied to Architecture*, one needs at least ten or more definers to capture anything as complex and statistical as a whole period. I have given thirty variables, in the charts that follow, definers that vary from ideology to style to design ideas – any one of which (such as Robert Venturi's 'complexity and contradiction') could be the subject of a whole book and mini-movement.

Given this heterogeneity, which is almost bewildering in its profusion, three points should be made. The classification of any architect within one tradition rather than another will be a matter of degree – a question of counting and weighing many variables, not just one or two; traditions resemble complex, multiform, organic entities which are fuzzy like neural networks rather than precise like military manoeuvres; and the critic must elucidate the rich profusion of species and genera while still distinguishing the few main phyla: Neo-, Late- and Post-Modern architecture as well as traditional building. Obviously unlike an animal an architect can, and often does, jump from one species to another while by and large remaining faithful to an overall approach. It is this relative consistency which makes classification possible, if fuzzy at points.

Rethinking Modernism – 'Modern-Next'

In addition to the writings and buildings of Eisenman and some other Deconstructionists, the architect who, through his work and theory, has most clearly defined the New Modern is the Japanese architect Kazuo Shinohara. In a key text of 1988 called 'Chaos and Machine' he gives it the strange appellation 'Modern-Next'. It is worth quoting from this text extensively as well as illustrating his Tokyo Institute of Technology Centennial Hall, for together they convey the new paradigm most clearly.

Shinohara, born in 1925, is part of the generation of architects who formed the Metabolist Movement in the 1960s, although slightly older. Like them he has explored many attitudes towards mechanical imagery, primitivism and tradition, but in his most recent 'fourth style' these concerns reach maturity. A key point was reached in 1987 when he finally became convinced of an earlier thesis, the idea that the new, information-oriented city, Tokyo, naturally expressed 'chaos', or as he also termed it 'The Beauty of Progressive Anarchy'

Chaos is a basic condition of the city ... Modernism, which had come via the United States, was becoming Japanised. Optimistic, technologically-oriented urban projects with huge concrete structures were popular among young architects. The architects dreamed of Japanese versions of Le Corbusier's 'La Ville Radieuse' ... However, I believed that it was impossible to create a city through a unified system ... In the last one or two years, people have shown increasing interest in Tokyo. Many people use as a working principle the idea that a confused, disorderly city is attractive. Various people have begun to

talk about the attractiveness, that is the 'beauty' of Tokyo, including those that only a few years ago were calling Tokyo nothing but a giant village.

Although Shinohara alludes here to the economic and social theories of Jane Jacobs – which are of course foundation ideas of Post-Modernism – he does not directly connect this chaotic, anarchistic beauty to the growth of small businesses and the economy. Nevertheless the connection exists and Shinohara intuitively understands that urban vitality and economic dynamism must mean visual anarchy and, as he calls it, 'the collection of an infinite number of urban functions' (instead of the Modernist reduction to four or five purified functions – work, habitation, circulation, recreation). Again following Jane Jacobs, he sees these 'infinite functions' as subsuming mixed uses and overlapping cultures, but adds to these notions the ideas of Chaos science, and the current interest in fractals and fluctuating systems which characterise all life.

Tokyo, the backward 'giant village' ... had never committed itself to the modernist vision of an industrial society but had instead leapfrogged that stage and had begun to demonstrate its unique qualities with the emergence of an information-oriented society. Chaos is not the result of poverty in Japanese cities today. Economic and social prosperity is evident in the commercial and entertainment centres of Tokyo. However, in terms of the visual environment composed of forms, colours, and materials, Tokyo is probably one of the most chaotic cities in the world. One can see, nevertheless, that in each individual building or urban facility, effort has been expended to provide order by one means or another.

Shinohara goes on to point out the mixture of order and chaos in building regulations and high technology, where geometry and control at a micro level are balanced by randomness and 'noise' on a macro scale; it is precisely this mixture he calls 'progressive anarchy' and seeks to represent in his architecture. He grants at once that those who hold to classical and modern canons of beauty will not find this chaos, or Tokyo, beautiful because they lack the unity and memory which are essential in virtually all aesthetic systems; but these absences are, for him, an essential part of the 'Modern-Next'.

Another part is the way that organisms, and higher level machines like computers have a built-in flexibility that can deal with randomness and fluctuation:

The study of chaotic phenomena is a new area of mathematics and physics. It is concerned with 'disorder, instability, variety, heterogeneity, and temporality'. Every system (of life) possesses a subsystem that 'fluctuates', to use Prigogines' expression ... It is impossible to predict whether the system will disintegrate into 'chaos' or become a 'dissipative structure' on a more differentiated and advanced level of organisation. This is because more energy is required to maintain the structure than the previous, simpler structure.

Shinohara then reiterates that he is not interested in 'unlimited chaos', but rather the kind of fluctuating, geometrical chaos that is evident in such advanced technology as the lunar spacecraft, and the most sophisticated fighter plane – the F14A Tomcat – both of which have awkward-looking movable parts. His Centennial Hall is meant to recall such flying machines, especially the stainless steel half cylinder that smashes through the abstract volumes and hovers in the air like the truncated wing of a 747. This is one type of 'geometrical form that fluctuates'.

Another type is the implicit 'lines of reference in plan', the axes set up within primary volumes – 90, 45, 30 degrees – and the slight deviation from these. Together both sets of axes form a new 'bundle of relationships between function and form that

PETER EISENMAN, WEXNER CENTER, COLUMBUS, OHIO

characterise organic and high-technological mechanisms ... these elements are juxtaposed so that a new bundle of relationships including fluctuation and randomness is generated among them'.

Shinohara concludes his text by pointing out how this new approach adds to Modernism the ideas of chaos, random noise, information exchange and a complex 'bundle of relationships' that is getting 'more and more difficult to see'. Although we may not be able to perceive his implicit geometric orders, we can easily see their complex 'difficulty' and also the emphasis on Modernist technology and the machine – both of which lead him to his goal, the 'Modern-Next'. In visual terms the results are close to the work of Frank Gehry and the Deconstructionists.

The Centennial Hall is a perfect illustration of Shinohara's theories. The juxtaposition of fragmented pure geometrics – the square, trapezoid, half-cylinder – generate the random noise which reflects the train station and urban chaos to the east, the messy jumble of telephone and electrical cables, the anarchic street signage, the random coming and going of grey aluminium trains and shining automobiles, all that urban reality condemned by Modernists in the pages of the *Architectural Review* as 'The Mess That is Man Made America', or the Modernist Peter Blake as *God's Own Junkyard*. This representation of mess is indeed the antithesis of the urban harmony which Le Corbusier and mega-structural designers of the 1960s had been promoting, but it is brought to a poetic intensity not found in the undesigned street environment where collisions just happen. Interestingly enough these juxtapositions and the inverted half-cylinder vaguely recall Le Corbusier's Ronchamp with its upturned and sagging roof. In its way the building has a comparable memorialising function to this church although here it is the progress of technology, not religion, which is being celebrated.

Formally and structurally the half-cylinder is a typical word of the Neo-Mods. Like the 'anti-gravitational architecture' of Zaha Hadid this form is a conceptual 'flying beam' that hovers out over space. Shinohara has conceived it as the symbol of 'a machine floating in the air', an airplane wing or fuselage, but it is equally illustrative of the 'suspended satellites' and 'explosive cantilevers' of Deconstructionist aesthetics. Like most Decon work it is bent – here in the middle, in plan, to connect visually the train station and chaotic city to the heart of the campus. And its cylindrical purity is further distorted and violated by a dissonantly curved window and 'flying' escape stairway. Here and elsewhere is the 'violated perfection', the rhetorical figure which at one time was the title of the first Deconstructivist Exhibition at the Museum of Modern Art

On the inside this 'flying beam' is the long tube-like corridor one finds at airports with walls that slope away from one and an underbelly that presses down into conference and conversation rooms below. One might feel slightly giddy in these warped and compressive spaces were it not for the muted pallette of greys and thick pile carpet. It's not unlike a fun-house at the circus, except the floors are flat and the sustained mood is austere. Deconstructionist architects, such as Eisenman, would no doubt have tilted the ground plane but also kept to the high-minded spectrum of silvers, greys, blacks and whites. In this sense the Neo-Mods remain Still-Modernists – intellectuals who contemplate the frenzy of street life rather than vulgarians who descend into it.

The characteristic hallmarks of the neo-modernist style are everywhere evident. Perforated aluminium panels, a favourite material, are gridded and then sectioned at an angle. Other rectangular panels jump up in steps or get sliced at sixty degrees. All pure volumes fly into each other with an awkward dissonance that suggests a rather impressive collision between two 747s. This explosive quality is as anti-classical as can be, since

parts are attached in 'an impromptu manner' and are intended not to make up a whole image. It sounds violent and uncontrolled, the architectural equivalent of a sixties Happening, but this violence is also mediated by a pervasive austerity and abstraction. Indeed Kazuo Shinohara is not the wilful romantic one might expect from reading this description, but a modest, retiring professor as unassuming in manner as he is scrupulous in thought. Because he has really thought through the implications of Modernism and recent developments in Chaos science, urban reality and biology, his Centennial Hall stands out as the most convincing example of Neo-Modernism. This is not to say it doesn't have the problems of this approach – an over-emphasis on abstraction, chaos and hard surfaces – but rather that these faults are marginalised by such a perfectly controlled explosion.

The New-Modern Corpus

How do we judge such work? Eisenman and Tschumi have, from time to time, followed a certain Deconstructionist argument which holds that good and bad, like all standards, are relative to a culture and ultimately meaningless. This position, which as good Deconstructionists they also contradict, would make discrimination virtually impossible. Yet judgement continues, and Shinohara continues to speak of 'beauty' as if it were meaningful not as harmony, but as a fuzzy sort of notion ('fuzzy theory' is as important as Chaos theory). In conversation he mentioned the beauty of fractals and difference, two notions which Eisenman also supports under the labels of 'self-similarity' and 'otherness'. There is indeed a growing neo-modern metalanguage that justifies and directs this architecture, a constellation of related terms which allows the designer to discriminate between permissible and wrong moves (although the idea of a 'mistake' is left very fuzzy). When on separate occasions, I asked both Shinohara and Eisenman how they would discriminate good from bad architecture, the answers were very ambiguous – not to say evasive. I presume, however, they make distinctions all the time and that these relate to the overall neo-modern corpus, summarised here in a diagram of thirty variables to relate to the other forms of Modernism.

This lexicon of stylistic terms, design ideas and norms is drawn from a wide variety of sources – notably Deconstructionist theory and the writings of Eisenman, Shinohara, Koolhaas, Hadid, Tschumi and Libeskind. It is representative rather than complete, but it gives a fair composite picture of what the new architect is up to – an ideal type Neo-Modernist rather than any real one. What kind of generalised portrait emerges?

The ideal type Neo-Mod will, ideologically speaking, displace the question of what style he or she is using as silly or reductive, and only admit to operating between styles. The reason for this, following the allusive arguments of Derrida, is that all categories are slippery and subject to contradictions and it is the job of the architect to 'deconstruct from within' the assumptions and styles which exist, to 'reinscribe' values and operate with the antinomy 'deconstruction/reconstruction', as Tschumi puts it. This makes their architecture ambiguous, like Post-Modernist work, but not in accord with the tastes and values of the local inhabitants.

Indeed, New Modern architecture is usually based on hermetic or private codes. A good example of this hermeticism is Peter Eisenman's social housing in Berlin which represents all sorts of interesting things such as the eighteenth-century past, the Berlin Wall, the adjacent buildings and their mutual collision. The only problem is that no one could decode these meanings unless they had an Eisenman text in hand. It is true the 3 3 metre base now has written on it the words 'Checkpoint Charlie' referring to the traumatic transition point just in back, but this was added by a sign artist intent on making Eisenman's architecture communicative. He, instead, just varies the size of abstract grids ('self-

I M PEI, JACOB K JAVITIS CENTRE

similarity'), sets them at an angle to each other, and then colours them light green, white, grey and red. In his hermetic code the green grid represents the adjacent nineteenth-century building and the angled white, red and grey grid represents the Berlin Wall and Mercator grid of the world, but no one would know this unless they were told. In fact many Berliners to whom I have talked misread the building as a jolly example of Post-Modern decoration – an interpretation which must be extremely painful to Eisenman who dislikes this tradition.

The ideal-type Neo-Modernist characteristically uses an asemantic form where there is a dissociation between form and content – the Berlin Wall represented by the incongruously cheerful grid of staggered windows. Also this type of architect will base his autonomous creations on metaphysical suppositions concerned with the 'end of architecture', an apocalyptic metaphysics which stems from the Holocaust, the Atom bomb, and the destructive aspects of modernisation and Modernism – that is, the harnessing of instrumental reason not to the project of the Enlightenment but to the forces of darkness.

This strong anti-modern streak in the New Modernism is best illustrated by the cryptic writings and projects of Daniel Libeskind. They are, he says, 'not theories' and 'not architecture'. Like Leon Krier, who has exerted a tremendous influence through not building his visions, Libeskind has had a profound influence with pure projects that are not contaminated by realisation. His models and drawings take much of the neo-modern aesthetic to an extreme as a frenzied cacophony of 'cocktail sticks', 'flying beams', 'excavations', 'tilted floors and walls', and 'self-contradictory inscriptions'. All of this is put to an apocalyptic end. It represents a new style of building 'not for the victors who have dominated architecture for five thousand years, but the vanquished – an architecture for losers'. Virtually all of the New Moderns have been haunted by Libeskind's uncompromising and incomprehensible 'otherness'.

The feeling of an alien landscape is inherent in the Modernist drive towards the unknown, the new and the 'next' and much Neo-Modernism shows this same attitude of estrangement. Like High-Tech architecture it insists on using products which have never been seen before. Even where Late-Modernists use a familiar glass and steel combination, they will stretch the slenderness ratios to new limits and produce unfamiliar proportions. Norman Foster's use of fuzzy glass with white dots to produce a gradation of light and visibility is a typical case. The familiar proportions of solid to void, spandrel to window, are melted into each other to create a curtain wall that seems to glow with a radioactive halo of shimmering particles.

Jean Nouvel, when he isn't being semantic and Post-Modern, will also use High-Tech in an abnormal way which recalls the proportions of Japanese architecture, very small buildings and even furniture. Both Foster and Nouvel, like the Neo-Modernists, enjoy the extreme repetition of prefabricated elements perhaps as much for their mesmerising otherness as for the cost. When a pure form is repeated *ad nauseum* it is not only monotonous but sublime, especially if it is beautifully detailed. In their insistence on the alien, the Late- and Neo-Modernists clearly share a common norm.

One important difference, however, is the value given to humour. A New Modernist, such as Frank Gehry, will abjure the old commitment to consistency and high-seriousness as he combines one technology with another in a way that defies logic. The *non sequitur*, the odd conjunction of 'fish and snake' shapes, the comic destruction of customary shapes, are made even odder and funnier by their warp and distortion. Peter Eisenman has introduced the same tactic with his 'banana' concept – the gratuitous form which results from intersecting two systems and representing this positively. Clearly the Neo-Mods have responded to the Post-Modern critique and also brought humour back to architecture.

This all too brief portrait of the ideal type New Modern illustrates only a few of the thirty variables shown in the diagram, but it suggests the key ideas. The typical architect will take a few elements from all the previous traditions including the rejected one, Post-Modernism. He or she will not really deal with the post-modern critique of urban anomie, destruction or deracination – except by intensifying it.

Bernard Tschumi's Parc de la Villette is characteristic in this respect since it is built of three discontinuous systems ('point grids', 'cinematic promenades' and 'surfaces') which are meant to reflect the non-place sprawl of suburbia, the de-regulation of free enterprise, the de-composition and de-centring of a society in flux. Not for him utopia, these *folies* are everyday reality turned into fire-engine-red machines that relate to nothing – except themselves and Neo-Constructivism. The hedonism and gratuity of this gesture is breath-taking, especially since the Parc already has one really expensive folly – a sixty million dollar meat market that never opened, but instead has been turned into a Museum of Science and Technology. Tschumi's pavilions declare their uselessness and atemporality with a panache that Modernists and functionalists would have found shocking. This is one more reason why, as opposed to many architects, I would never call these architects 'Modern'. They have fundamentally extended and distorted the paradigm of the 1920s.

Modernism as the Style and Religion of the Bourgeoisie

Let us step back from the argument so far and take a wider look at the way Modernism has developed through all its changes over the last 150 years and yet retained certain assumptions and a general direction. In this broader perspective I'll make use of some ideas developed in the 1980s while New Modernism was in the process of formation, above all the most important reconsideration of Modernism by Marshall Berman, *All That is Solid Melts into Air*, subtitled 'The Experience of Modernity' first published in 1982. No thorough discussion of modernity can take place today without being informed by this book, although its implications may be misunderstood even by the author himself.

Berman develops the argument of his title that Modernity is essentially involved with evanescence, continual change, rapid obsolescence, constant revolution – and this title comes from Karl Marx's *The Communist Manifesto*:

Constant revolutionising of production, uninterrupted disturbance of all social relations, everlasting uncertainty and agitating, distinguish the bourgeois epoch from all earlier times. All fixed, fast-frozen relationships, with their train of venerable ideas and opinions, are swept away, all new-formed ones become obsolete before they can ossify. All that is solid melts into air, all that is holy is profaned, and men at last are forced to face with sober senses the real conditions of their lives and relations with their fellow men.

The inventive reading Berman gives to this, and Marx in general, is to turn *The Communist Manifesto* of 1848 into 'the first great modernist work of art' and, as if that weren't a radical enough notion, show that Marx actually celebrated the destructive change brought about by capitalism and the bourgeoisie. Secondly, and just as importantly, Berman connects up modernisation with Modernism. This may seem an obvious pairing, and every textbook on Modern architecture makes it in a general way, but Berman brings out its dark side, the continual destruction necessitated by industrial innovation and relentless change, the nihilism inherent in wiping away neighbourhoods and the past. Previously, apologists for Modernism – and Berman turns out to be one – had underplayed the Faustian bargain struck by

TADAO ANDO, CHAPEL ON MOUNT ROKKO, KOBE, HYOGO

developers and Modernists between destruction and creation and only accentuated the progressive side. With Faust and Marx as his main characters, however, Berman makes clear that over a 200 year period modernisation and its ideology of Modernism are tragically implicated in the annihilation of ethnic domain, roots or anything that stands in the way of the bourgeoisie. The Faustian power of capitalism 'melts all that is solid into air' and Modernism is *the* style and religion of this incandescent force.

With this fundamental insight in mind we can begin to understand the schizophrenia and pathology of Modernists, who celebrate continual revolution but have a guilty conscience about the inevitable destruction entailed – even of themselves. The bourgeoisie, Berman points out, have to hide this guilt:

> Their secret – a secret they have managed to keep even from themselves – is that, behind their façades, they are the most violently destructive ruling class in history. All the anarchic, measureless, explosive drives that a later generation will baptise by the name of 'nihilism' – drives that Nietzsche and his followers will ascribe to such cosmic traumas as the Death of God – are located by Marx in the seemingly banal everyday working of the market economy. He unveils the modern bourgeois as consummate nihilists on a vaster scale than modern intellectuals can conceive.

This secret of the Modernist and bourgeois alike helps explain the self-destructive streak which runs through modern movements over two hundred years, the constant return to the blank canvas, ground zero, the *tabula rasa*; it helps explain why these various movements last barely ten years in the nineteenth century, and a mere two years today. The quick substitution of 'isms' – all the fashions which become 'wasms' – shows the dark secret which Modernists can never admit to themselves – their art movements *are* fashions, their class identity is bourgeois. This last secret is the most disturbing of all and must be denied at all costs behind a succession of anti-bourgeois slogans (*épater les bourgeois*) and anti-middle-class styles.

Nietzsche faces this ambivalent truth as clearly as Marx and in the famous lines from *Thus Spoke Zaratnustra*, he sings the praises of the new superman, the destructive creator:

He who must be a creator in good and evil – verily, he must first be a destroyer, and break values into pieces. Thus the highest evil is part of the highest goodness. But that s creative goodness. Let us speak thereon, ye wisest men, however bad it be. To be silent is worse; all unuttered truths become poisonous. And whatever will break on our truths, let it break! Many a house hath yet to be built. Thus spake Zarathustra.

Le Corbusier was the architect most affected by these cruel truths which he read as a young man in Paris in 1908. He might have noticed the phrase 'many a house hath yet to be built', but in any case he later proposed the destruction of Paris' historic centre and its creative replacement by glass and steel towers dedicated to the new supermen – businessmen, 'captains of industry' as he kept calling them, the new leaders of the bourgeoisie. In a letter of 1908 to his teacher and guru Charles l'Eplattenier, he adopts the Nietzschean rhetoric – 'burn what you love, love what you burn' – and then for the rest of his ceaselessly creative life carries out this destructive creation, firing his architectural office every seven years or so, changing styles and approach every ten years; even in the 1920s changing his name several times.

There is no doubt that Le Corbusier saw himself as the Nietzschean future man dedicating himself to 'transvaluing all values', overcoming the mediocrity of mass culture, and turning himself into a kind of creative superhero – painting in the morning, city planning and architecting in the afternoon, writing at night. Through will-power and hard work he, like Picasso and Duchamp and other Modernists, became the ultimate bourgeois –

the self-developed over-achiever, the widely-balanced hero of Marx's Communist utopia, the man who could do everything. Had jogging been fashionable, he would have run marathons.

The culture of Modernism, with its litany of super-saints and creative giants, its roll-call of new orthodoxies and schisms, has no doubt become a religion – or perhaps pseudo-religion is the better word since it is also applied to Marxism, nationalism, the cult of self-development and other secular creeds. The way Modernism has become an ideology and faith since Nietzsche proclaimed the Death of God has been noted before, but I'm not sure whether the stylistic and iconographic implications of this shift have been observed. Adolf Loos, in the early part of this century, formulates a reason for the chaste international style which will be without ornament. In his polemic *Architecture*, 1910, he laments the fact that the architect 'possesses no culture', unlike the peasant or Papuan rooted in a tradition, and therefore will draw whimsical ornament and adopt false, fashionable styles. The architect is the quintessential bourgeois: 'Like almost every town dweller,' Loos writes, 'the architect possesses no culture. He does not have the security of the peasant to whom the culture is innate. The town dweller is an upstart.' The cure for this, Loos makes clear in his writings and buildings, is an abstract, white, geometric style which is based on functions and understated in appearance – like the proverbial silent butler in British theatre.

Overall he gives a powerful, cumulative argument that the new bourgeoisie, as opposed to the aristocracy and peasantry, has no valuative system and thus, like Nietzsche's superman, has to invent one *ex nihilo* based on utility, strength through competition and higher-order abstract perception – like listening to Beethoven's symphonies. With hindsight it is easier to say that this cultural Modernism has become *the* style of the bourgeoisie and that among its many formal variants Loos' stripped functionalism, the zero-degree abstraction, has become the leading mode. This white abstract style represents, at once, good taste, the healthy life that appealed to Loos, Le Corbusier, Voysey and Lethaby – that is skiing, tennis, aerobics, holidays in the mountains and by the sea – and the liberation from the past, the aristocracy, eclecticism and, most importantly, the guilt of continual destruction. All of these historical overtones are purged and the new city is prepared as a clean white slate ready for redevelopment. This *tabula rasa* is of course to be controlled by the new class – that is, the combination of bureaucrats, government officials and corporate leaders who have dominated city life from London to New York, from the Docklands to Battery Park City.

To an extent which would have pleased Adolf Loos these upstarts and yuppies have thrown off most of the knick-knacks and superficial historicism of their nineteenth-century forbears and embraced an abstract, timeless, utilitarian style – although like most other classes today they still decorate their houses with traditional elements. Confident and unsentimental about roots, willing to sacrifice almost anything for economic and technological progress, they have created huge, abstract monuments which are so typical of today's commerce – the shopping centre, or, even more, the gigantic convention centre which might have up to six major exhibition spaces. As Peter Eisenman predicts, the convention centre is set to become the building type of the nineties, a replacement for that of the eighties, the museum.

That Modernists evolved a chaste style which rejected their bourgeois roots is a thesis argued with force and irony by Tom Wolfe in *From Bauhaus to Our House*, 1981. Noting the way the Bauhaus and the glass and steel blocks of the Avenue of the Americas in New York resemble ideal socialist schemes, he draws the following conclusions:

First the new architecture was being created for the workers. The holiest of all goals: perfect worker housing. Second, the new architecture was to reject all things bourgeois. Since just about everyone involved, the architects as well as the Social Democrat bureaucrats, was himself bourgeois in the literal, social sense of the word, 'bourgeois' became an epithet that meant whatever you didn't like in the lives of people above the level of hod carrier. The main thing was not to be caught designing something someone could point to and say of, with a devastating sneer: 'How very bourgeois'.

As Wolfe notes, the working class has nearly always disliked the white abstractions made in their name and preferred to live in something more polychromatic and exuberant.

Putting together Marx, Loos, Wolfe and Berman we may summarise an argument: all periods of history have a unique style or set of modes, and the new, bourgeois class has a distinctive style based on the antinomy 'destruction/creation'. Because this class is without strong roots and culture, it develops an abstract geometric style where, if there is any ornament, it will consist in such utilitarian things as structure. This timeless mode rejects not only history but its social genesis, the bourgeoisie itself, as it embraces the vision of a utopian working class – a proletariat that has never existed, but one which will be without self-interest, difference, bad taste, and individuality.

But why should the bourgeoisie be so relentlessly anti-bourgeois? Why should the Modernist do everything to deny his social background? (There are far fewer female Modernists than male.) Is it that he can't face the destruction inherent in development, the deracination and cultural annihilation which Marx and Nietzsche expose? The fact that all new Modernisms, for two hundred years, must deny their predecessors, throw their ancestors on the 'scrap-heap of history' as the Futurists proposed for each generation, and suppress their own identity, their own tradition? The fact that Modernism is, culturally speaking, suicidal?

Something like this must explain the constant reappearance of destructive imagery, of Brutalist and minimalist styles which recur in a new guise – as Classicism used to do – every twenty years. In this sense Modernism is nothing else than the bourgeois denying his own existence, a destruction turned tragically inwards. We find many echoes of this from Le Corbusier's constant invocation to 'start again from zero', to Roland Barthes' anti-bourgeois degree-zero style; from the constant death and rebirth of the avant-garde to the metaphor of the phoenix, from the attacks on consumerism, ornament and representation, to the advocacy of a counter-style which is supposedly unconsumable – too difficult for the middle-class to swallow.

The New Moderns continually make this last opposition as they insist on their purity and anti-populism, their avoidance of contamination by commerce. Kenneth Frampton's defense of Tadao Ando's architecture – which is itself firmly based on Le Corbusier's degree-zero style – is the archetype.

... Ando's architecture is critical in the sense that it resists being absorbed into the ever-escalating consumerism of the modern city ... Ando has stoically refused the nostalgic ethos which such vernacular elements display ... Ando values the 'silence' of modern form for its resistance to consumption ... when it comes to the evaluation of functional forms, Ando remains opposed to both bourgeois comfort and the ideals of ergonomic convenience, since for him such criteria are contaminated by consumerism.

This renunciation sounds plausible at first, and Frampton drives home his message by calling Ando's work 'subversive'; but then one notes the conventional nature of this purgation and stoic silence, the way it follows the customary modernist pattern of renunciation, and it only takes another second of reflection to realise that Ando, like Le Corbusier before him, has become the focus for new wave fashion – indeed fashion photographers – and even more well-known internationally than those architects who are more accessible, representational or nostalgic. Ché Guevara's revolutionary purity was turned into a consumerist product, and the Modernist pure of heart suffers this success too. The really bourgeois styles today are always anti-bourgeois.

This detour to a form of psycho-history brings us back to patterns that still remain in the New Modernism, the most constant of which is the New seen as something alien or 'other'. 'Make it strange' is a constant romantic injunction of two hundred years, a command which necessitates the constant paradoxical destruction of the 'Tradition of the New'. Forgetfulness is an important mental skill to cultivate and it is no surprise that our quintessential New Mod, Peter Eisenman, has made an acrostic from his name – 'amnesia'. Always churning out new figures of speech and visual tropes from his rhetoric machine, he constantly moves ground that covers familiar ground, from 'anti-memory' to 'dissimulation', 'catachresis', 'arabesques' and so on through thirty or more terms. Each one extends his architecture in small ways giving it life, keeping it free from cliché and repetition, and yet each one recalls the constant return of the Modern to abstraction, the 'other' and destruction/construction.

The creative transformation of old/new Modernism is no small matter in an era when so much architecture, produced by large firms, has become predictable. 'The Life of Forms in Art', Henri Focillon's phrase, is to be respected just as the goal of the Modernists – self-development – has its point.

If there is an obvious problem to the New Modernism it is its extreme hermeticism, the lack of a social basis and wide appeal, the inability to be understood except by a small coterie. Also the architecture over-emphasises chaos, as if every event in the universe were a thunderstorm rather than more predictable weather. In the 1960s a 'real' Modern architect, Mies van der Rohe, decreed – 'you can't make a new architecture every Monday morning'. The New Moderns, true to the demonic strain in their tradition, replied – 'Oh, but you can, and *that* is the point of Modernism. There's not much else for a Modernist to be.'

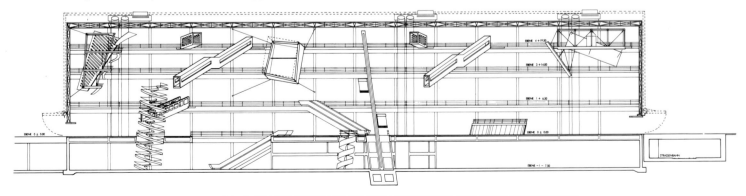

BERNARD TSCHUMI, ZKM CENTRE FOR ART AND MEDIA TECHNOLOGY, KARLSRUHE, WEST GERMANY

KENNETH FRAMPTON

RAPPEL A L'ORDRE: THE CASE FOR THE TECTONIC

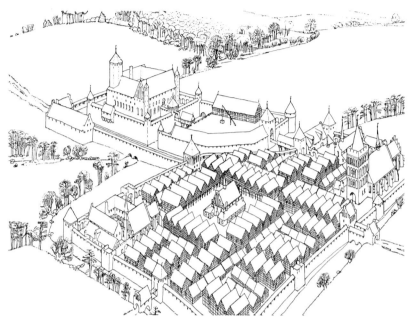

IDEAL VIEW OF A MEDIAEVAL TOWN FROM *DIE GESTALT DER DEUTSCHEN STADT* BY KARL GRUBER 1937

I have elected to address the issue of tectonic form for a number of reasons, not least of which is the current tendency to reduce architecture to scenography. This reaction arises in response to the universal triumph of Robert Venturi's decorated shed; that all too prevalent syndrome in which shelter is packaged like a giant commodity. Among the advantages of the scenographic approach is

the fact that the results are eminently amortisable with all the consequences that this entails for the future of the environment. We have in mind, of course, not the pleasing decay of 19th-century Romanticism but the total destitution of commodity culture. Along with this sobering prospect goes the general dissolution of stable references in the late-modern world; the fact that the precepts governing almost every discourse, save for the seemingly autonomous realm of techno-science, have now become extremely tenuous. Much of this was already foreseen half a century ago by Hans Sedlmayr, when he wrote, in 1941:

> The shift of man's spiritual centre of gravity towards the inorganic, his feeling of his way into the inorganic world may indeed legitimately be called a cosmic disturbance in the microcosm of man, who now begins to show a one-sided development of his faculties. At the other extreme there is a disturbance of macrocosmic relationships, a result of the especial favour and protection which the inorganic now enjoys – almost always at the expense, not to say ruin, of the inorganic. The raping and destruction of the earth, the nourisher of man, is an obvious example and one which in its turn reflects the distortion of the human microcosm for the spiritual.[1]

Against this prospect of cultural degeneration we may turn to certain rearguard positions, in order to recover a basis from which to resist. Today we find ourselves in a similar position to

that of the critic Clement Greenberg who, in his 1965 essay 'Modernist Painting', attempted to reformulate a ground for painting in the following terms:

> Having been denied by the Enlightenment of all tasks they could take seriously, they (the arts) looked as though they were going to be assimilated to entertainment pure and simple, and entertainment itself looked as though it were going to be assimilated, like religion, to therapy. The arts could save themselves from this levelling down only by demonstrating that the kind of experience they provided was valuable in its own right, and not to be obtained from any other kind of activity.[2]

If one poses the question as to what might be a comparable ground for architecture, then one must turn to a similar material base, namely that architecture must of necessity be embodied in structural and constructional form. My present stress on the latter rather than the prerequisite of spatial enclosure stems from an attempt to evaluate 20th-century architecture in terms of continuity and inflection rather than in terms of originality as an end in itself.

In his 1980 essay, 'Avant Garde and Continuity', the Italian architect Giorgio Grassi had the following comment to make about the impact of avant-gardist art on architecture

> . . . as far as the vanguards of the Modern Movement are concerned, they invariably follow in the wake of the

figurative arts ... Cubism, Suprematism, Neoplasticism, etc, are all forms of investigation born and developed in the realm of the figurative arts, and only as a second thought carried over into architecture as well. It is actually pathetic to see the architects of that 'heroic' period and the best among them, trying with difficulty to accommodate themselves to these 'isms'; experimenting in a perplexed manner because of their fascination with the new doctrines, measuring them, only later to realise their ineffectuality ...[3]

While it is disconcerting to have to recognise that there may well be a fundamental break between the figurative origins of abstract art and the constructional basis of tectonic form, it is, at the same time, liberating to the extent that it affords a point from which to challenge spatial invention as an end in itself: a pressure to which modern architecture has been unduly subject. Rather than join in a recapitulation of avant-gardist tropes or enter into historicist pastiche or into the superfluous proliferation of sculptural gestures all of which have an arbitrary dimension to the degree that they are based in neither structure nor in construction, we may return instead to the structural unit as the

cific media which determine not only aesthetic choices but also the ethical content of its cultural contribution. Through these channels of ethical and political will, the concern of the Enlightenment ... becomes enriched in its most critical tone. It is not solely the superiority of reason and the analysis of form which are indicated, but rather, the critical role (in the Kantian sense of the term) that is, the judgement of values, the very lack of which is felt in society today ...
In the sense that his architecture is a meta-language, a reflection on the contradictions of its own practice, his work acquires the appeal of something that is both frustrating and noble ...

The dictionary definition of the term 'tectonic' to mean 'pertaining to building or construction in general; constructional, constructive used especially in reference to architecture and the kindred arts,' is a little reductive to the extent that we intend not only the structural component *in se* but also the formal amplification of its presence in relation to the assembly of which it is a part. From its conscious emergence in the middle of the 19th century with the writings of Karl Bottischer and Gottfried Semper the term not only indicates a structural and material

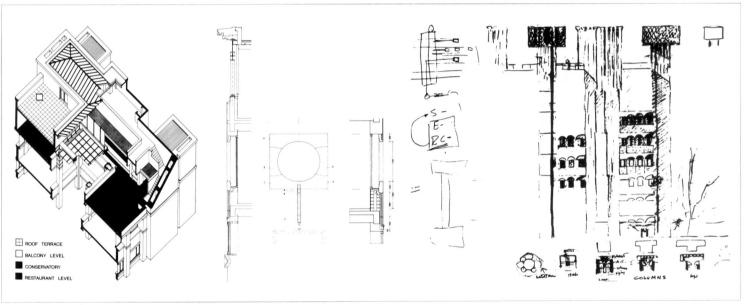

L TO R: F. LLOYD WRIGHT, LARKIN BUILDING, AXONOMETRIC OF FIFTH FLOOR; C SCARPA, BANCO POPOLARE DI VERONA; LOUIS KAHN, RICHARDS' LABORATORIES, PHILADELPHIA

irreducible essence of architectural form.

Needless to say, we are not alluding here to mechanical revelation of construction but rather to a potentially poetic manifestation of structure in the original Greek sense of *poesis* as an act of making and revealing. While I am well aware of the conservative connotations that may be ascribed to Grassi's polemic, his critical perceptions none the less cause us to question the very idea of the new, in a moment that oscillates between the cultivation of a resistant culture and a descent into value-free aestheticism. Perhaps the most balanced assessment of Grassi has been made by the Catalan critic, Ignasi Sola Morales, when he wrote:

Architecture is posited as a craft, that is to say, as the practical application of established knowledge through rules of the different levels of intervention. Thus, no notion of architecture as problem-solving, as innovation, or as invention *ex novo,* is present in Grassi's thinking, since he is interested in showing the permanent, the evident, and the given character of knowledge in the making of architecture.
... The work of Grassi is born of a reflection upon the essential resources of discipline, and it focuses upon spe-

probity but also a poetics of construction, as this may be practised in architecture and the related arts.

The beginnings of the Modern, dating back at least two centuries, and the much more recent advent of the Post-Modern are inextricably bound up with the ambiguities introduced into Western architecture by the primacy given to the scenographic in the evolution of the bourgeois world. However, building remains essentially *tectonic* rather than scenographic in character and it may be argued that it is an act of construction first, rather than a discourse predicated on the surface, volume and plan, to cite the 'Three Reminders to Architects', of Le Corbusier. Thus one may assert that building is *ontological* rather than *representational* in character and that built form is a presence rather than something standing for an absence. In Martin Heidegger's terminology we may think of it as a 'thing' rather than a 'sign'.

I have chosen to engage this theme because I believe it is necessary for architects to re-position themselves given that the predominant tendency today is to reduce all architectural expression to the status of commodity culture. In as much as such resistance has little chance of being widely accepted, a 'rearguard' posture would seem to be an appropriate stance to adopt rather than the dubious assumption that it is possible to continue with the perpetuation of avant gardism. Despite its concern for structure, an emphasis on tectonic form does not necessarily favour either Constructivism or Deconstructivism. In this sense it is astylistic. Moreover it does not seek its legitimacy in science, literature or art.

Greek in origin, the term *tectonic* derives from the term *tekton,* signifying carpenter or builder. This in turn stems from the Sanskrit *taksan,* referring to the craft of carpentry and to the use of the ax. Remnants of a similar term can also be found in Vedic, where it again refers to carpentry. In Greek it appears in Homer, where it again alludes to carpentry and to the art of construction in general. The poetic connotation of the term first appears in Sappho where the *tekton,* the carpenter, assumes the role of the poet. This meaning undergoes further evolution as the term passes from being something specific and physical, such as carpentry, to the more generic notion of construction and later to becoming an aspect of poetry. In Aristophanes we even find the the idea that it is even associated with machination and the creation of false things. This etymological evolution would suggest a gradual passage from the ontological to the representa-

tectonic object, that appears in two modes. We may refer to these modes as the ontological and representational *tectonic.* The first involves a constructional element, that is shaped so as to emphasise its static role and cultural status. This is the tectonic as it appears in Bottischer's interpretation of the Doric column. The second mode involves the representation of a constructional element which is present, but hidden. These two modes can be seen as paralleling the distinction that Semper made between the *structural-technical* and the *structural-symbolic.*

Aside from these distinctions, Semper was to divide built form into two separate material procedures: into the *tectonics* of the frame in which members of varying lengths are conjoined to encompass a spatial field and the *stereotomics* of compressive mass that, while it may embody space, is constructed through the piling up of identical units; the term *sterotomics* deriving from the Greek term for solid, *stereos* and cutting, *-tomia.* In the first case, the most common material throughout history has been *wood* or its textual equivalents such as bamboo, wattle and basket-work. In the second case, one of the most common materials has been brick, or the compressive equivalent of brick such as rock, stone or rammed earth and later, reinforced

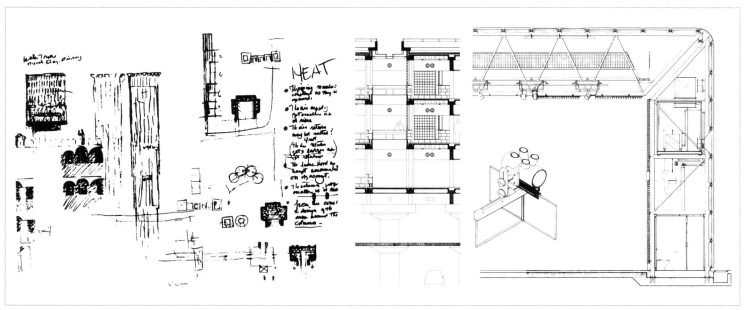

L TO R: LOUIS KAHN, RICHARDS LABORATORIES; N. FOSTER, SAINSBURY CENTRE, CROSS-SECTION OF DETAIL; HERMAN HERTZBERGER, CENTRAL BEHEER, APELDOORN, CROSS-SECTION

tional. Finally, the Latin term *architectus* derives from the Greek *archi* (a person of authority) and *tekton* (a craftsman or builder).

The earliest appearance of the term 'tectonic' in English dates from 1656 where it appears in a glossary meaning 'belonging to building', and this is almost a century after the first English use of the term *architect* in 1563. In 1850 the German oriental scholar K O Muller was to define the term rather rudely, as 'A series of arts which form and perfect vessels, implements, dwellings and places of assembly'. The term is first elaborated in a modern sense with Karl Bottischer's *The Tectonic of the Hellenes* of 1843-52 and with Gottfried Semper's essay *The Four Elements of Architecture* of the same year. It is further developed in Semper's unfinished study, *Style in the Technical and Tectonic Arts or Practical Aesthetic* published between 1863 and 1868.

The term 'tectonic' cannot be divorced from the technological, and it is this that gives a certain ambivalence to the term. In this regard it is possibly to identify three distinct conditions; (1) the *technological object* that arises directly out of meeting an instrumental need, (2) the *scenographic object* that may be used equally to allude to an absent or hidden element, and (3), the

concrete. There have been significant exceptions to this division particularly where, in the interest of permanence, stone has been cut, dressed, and erected in such a way as to assume the form and function of a frame. While these facts are so familiar as to hardly need repetition, we tend to be unaware of the ontological consequences of these differences; that is to say, of the way in which framework tends towards the aerial and the dematerialisation of mass, whereas the mass form is telluric, embedding itself ever deeper into the earth. The one tends towards light and the other towards dark. These gravitational opposites, the immateriality of the frame and the materiality of the mass, may be said to symbolise the two cosmological opposites to which they aspire; the sky and the earth. Despite our highly secularised techno-scientific age, these polarities still largely constitute the experiential limits of our lives. It is arguable that the practice of architecture is impoverished to the extent that we fail to recognise these transcultural values and the way in which they are intrinsically latent in all structural form. Indeed, these forms may serve to remind us, after Heidegger, that inanimate objects may also evoke 'being', and that through this analogy to our own corpus, the body of a building may be perceived as though it were literally a physique. This brings us back to Semper's privileging of the joint as the primordial tectonic element as the fundamental nexus around which building comes into being, that is to say, comes to be articulated as a presence in itself.

Semper's emphasis on the joint implies that fundamental syntactical transition may be expressed as one passes from the *stereotomic* base to the *tectonic* frame, and that such transitions constitute the very essence of architecture. They are the dominant constituents whereby one culture of building differentiates itself from the next.

There is a spiritual value residing in the particularities of a given joint that the 'thingness' of the constructed object, so much so that the generic joint becomes a point of ontological condensation rather than a mere connection. We need only to think of the work of Carlo Scarpa to touch on a contemporary manifestation of this attribute.

The first volume of the fourth edition of Karl Bottischer's *Tektonik der Hellenen* appeared in 1843, two years after Schinkel's death in 1841. This publication was followed by three subsequent volumes which appeared at intervals over the next decade, the last appearing in 1852, the year of Semper's *Four*

Bottischer was greatly influenced by the philosopher Josef von Schelling's view that architecture transcends the mere pragmatism of building by virtue of assuming symbolic significance. For Schelling and Bottischer alike, the inorganic had no symbolic meaning, and hence structural form could only acquire symbolic value by virtue of its capacity to engender analogies between tectonic and organic form. However, any kind of direct imitation of natural form was to be avoided since both men held the view that architecture was an imitative art only in so far as it imitated itself. This view tends to corroborate Grassi's contention that architecture has always been distanced from the figurative arts, even if its form can be seen as paralleling nature. In this capacity architecture simultaneously serves both as a metaphor of, and as a foil to, the naturally organic. In tracing this thought retrospectively, one may cite Semper's 'Theory of Formal Beauty' of 1856 in which he no longer grouped architecture with painting and sculpture as a plastic art, but with dance and music as a cosmic art, as an ontological world-making art rather than as representational form. Semper regarded such arts as paramount not only because they were symbolic but also because they embodied man's underlying erotic-ludic urge to strike a beat, to

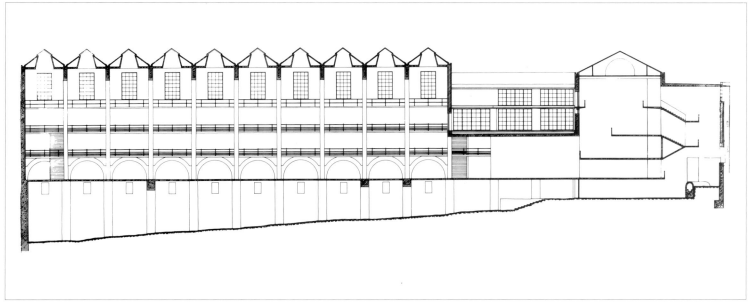

RAFAEL MONEO, ROMAN ARCHAEOLOGICAL MUSEUM, MERIDA, 1980-85, LONGIDUDINAL SECTION SHOWING EARTHWORK AND FOLDED MONITOR ROOF

Elements of Architecture. Bottischer elaborated the concept of the tectonic in a number of significant ways. At one level he envisaged a conceptual *juncture,* which came into being through the appropriate interlocking of constructional elements. Simultaneously articulated and integrated, these conjunctions were seen as constituting the body-form, the *Korperbilden* of the building that not only guaranteed its material finish of the building, but also enabled this function to be recognised, as a symbolic form. At another level, Bottischer distinguished between the *Kernform* or nucleus and the *Kunstform* or decorative cladding, the latter having the purpose of representing and symbolising the institutional status of the work. According to Bottischer, this shell or revetment had to be capable of revealing the inner essence of the tectonic nucleus. At the same time Bottischer insisted that one must always try to distinguish between the indispensable structural form and its enrichment, irrespective of whether the latter is merely the shaping of the technical elements as in the case of the Doric column or the cladding of its basic form with revetment. Semper will later adapt this notion of *Kunstform* to the idea of *Bekleidung,* that is to say, to the concept of literally 'dressing' the fabric of a structure.

string a necklace, to weave a pattern, and thus to decorate according to a rhythmic law.

Semper's *Four Elements of Architecture* of 1852 brings the discussion full circle in as much as Semper added a specific anthropological dimension to the idea of tectonic form. Semper's theoretical schema constitutes a fundamental break with the four hundred year old humanist formula of *utilitas, firmitas, venustas,* that first served as the intentional triad of Roman architecture and then as the underpinning of post-Vitruvian architectural theory. Semper's radical reformulation stemmed from his seeing a model of a Caribbean hut in the Great Exhibition of 1851. The empirical reality of this simple shelter caused Semper to reject Laugier's primitive hut, adduced in 1753 as the primordial form of shelter with which to substantiate the pedimented paradigm of Neoclassical architecture. Semper's Four Elements countermanded this hypothetical assumption and asserted instead an anthropological construct comprising (1) a hearth, (2) an earthwork, (3) a framework and a roof, and (4) an enclosing membrane.

While Semper's elemental model repudiated Neoclassical authority it none the less gave primacy to the frame over the loadbearing mass. At the same time, Semper's four part thesis recognised the primary importance of the earthwork, that is to say, of a telluric mass that serves in one way or another to anchor the frame or the wall, or Mauer, into the site.

This marking, shaping, and preparing of ground by means of an earthwork had a number of theoretical ramifications. On the one hand, it isolated the enclosing membrane as a differentiating act, so that the *textural* could be literally identified with the proto-linguistic nature of textile production that Semper regarded as the basis of all civilisation. On the other hand, as Rosemary Bletter has pointed out, by stressing the earthwork as the fundamental basic form, Semper gave symbolic import to a nonspatial element, namely, the hearth that was invariably an inseparable part of the earthwork. The term 'breaking ground' and the metaphorical use of the word 'foundation' are both obviously related to the primacy of the earthwork and the hearth.

In more ways than one Semper grounded his theory of architecture in a phenomenal element having strong social and spiritual connotations. For Semper the hearth's origin was linked to that of the altar, and as such it was the spiritual nexus of architectural form. The hearth bears within itself connotations in the female place of honour and the sun of the interior.[5] As is well known, there are etymological connotations residing here of which Semper was fully aware, above all, the connection between *knot* and *joint,* the former being in German *die Knoten* and the latter *die Naht.* In modern German both words are related to *die Verbindung,* which may be literally translated as 'the binding'. All this evidence tends to support Semper's contention that the ultimate constituent of the art of building is the joint.

The primacy that Semper accorded to the knot seems to be supported by Gunther Nitschke's research into Japanese binding and unbinding rituals as set forth in his seminal essay *Shi-Me* of 1979. In Shinto culture these proto-tectonic binding rituals constitute agrarian renewal rites. They point at once to that close association between building dwelling, cultivating, and being, remarked on by Martin Heidegger in his essay 'Building, Dwelling, Thinking' of 1954.

Semper's distinction between *tectonic* and *stereotonic* returns us to theoretical arguments recently advanced by the Italian architect Vittorio Gregotti, who proposes that the marking of ground, rather than the primitive hut, is the primordial tectonic act. In his 1983 address to the New York Architectural League,

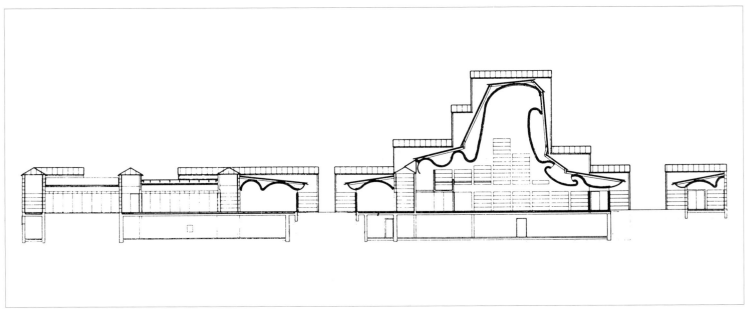

JORN UTZON, BAGSVAERD CHURCH, DENMARK, 1977, LONGITUDINAL SECTION

this regard. It derives from the Latin verb *aedisficare* which in its turn is the origin of the English word *edifice,* meaning literally 'to make a hearth'. The latent institutional connotations of both hearth and edifice are further suggested by the verb *to edify,* which means to educate, strengthen and instruct.

Influenced by linguistic and anthropological insights of his age, Semper was concerned with the etymology of building. Thus he distinguished the massivity of a fortified stone wall as indicated by the term *Mauer* from the light frame and infill, wattle and daub say, of mediaeval domestic building, for which the term *Wand* is used. This fundamental distinction has been nowhere more graphically expressed than in Karl Gruber's reconstruction of a mediaeval German town. Both *Mauer* and *Wand* reduce to the word 'wall' in English, but the latter in German is related to the word for dress, *Gewand,* and to the term *Winden,* which means to embroider. In accordance with the primacy that he gave to textiles, Semper maintained that the earliest basic structural artifact was the knot which predominates in nomadic building form, especially in the Bedouin tent and its textile interior. We may note here in passing Pierre Bourdieux's analysis of the Bedouin house wherein the loom is identified as

Gregotti stated:

> . . . The worst enemy of modern architecture is the idea of space considered solely in terms of its economic and technical exigencies indifferent to the idea of the site.
>
> The built environment that surrounds us is, we believe, the physical representation of its history, and the way in which it has accumulated different levels of meaning to form the specific quality of the site, *not* just for what it appears to be, in perceptual terms, but for what it is in structural terms.
>
> Geography is the description of how the signs of history have become forms, therefore the architectural project is charged with the task of revealing the essence of the geo-environmental context through the transformation of form. The environment is therefore not a system in which to dissolve architecture. On the contrary, it is the most important material from which to develop the project.
>
> Indeed, through the concept of the site and the principle of settlement, the environment becomes the essence of architectural production. From this vantage point, new principles and methods can be seen for design. Principles

23

and methods that give precedence to the siting in a specific area (sic). This is an act of knowledge of the context *that comes out of its architectural modification* (my italics). The origin of architecture is not the primitive hut, the cave or the mythical 'Adam's House in Paradise'. Before transforming a support into a column, roof into a tympanum, before placing stone on stone, man placed a stone on the ground to recognise a site in the midst of an unknown universe, in order to take account of it and modify it. As with every act of assessment, this one required radical moved and apparent simplicity. From this point of view, there are only two important attitudes to the context. The tools of the first are mimesis, organic imitation and the display of complexity. The tools of the second are the assessment of physical relations, formal definition and the interiorisation of complexity.[6]

With the tectonic in mind it is possible to posit a revised account of the history of modern architecture, for when the entire trajectory is reinterpreted through the lens of *techne* certain patterns emerge and others recede. Seen in this light a tectonic impulse may be traced across the century uniting diverse works irrespective of their different origins. In this process well-known affinities are further reinforced, while others recede and hitherto unremarked connections emerge asserting the importance of criteria that lie beyond superficial stylistic differences. Thus for all their stylistic idiosyncrasies a very similar level of tectonic articulation patently links Hendrik Petrus Berlage's Stock Exchange of 1895 to Frank Lloyd Wright's Larkin Building of 1904 and Herman Hertzberger's Central Beheer office complex of 1974. In each instance there is a similar concatenation of span and support that amounts to a tectonic syntax in which gravitational force passes from purlin to truss, to pad stone, to corbel, to arch, to pier and abutment. The technical transfer of this load passes through a series of appropriately articulated transitions and joints. In each of these works the constructional articulation engenders the spatial subdivision and vice versa and this same principle may be found in other works of this century possessing quite different stylistic aspirations. Thus we find a comparable concern for the revealed joint in the architecture of both August Perret and Louis Kahn. In each instance the joint guarantees the probity and presence of the overall form while alluding to distinct different ideological and referential antecedents. Thus where Perret looks back to the structurally rationalised classicism of the Graeco-Gothic ideal, dating back in France to the beginning of the 18th century, Kahn evokes a 'timeless archaism', at once technologically advanced but spiritually antique.

The case can be made that the prime inspiration behind all this work stemmed as much from Eugène Viollet-le-Duc as from Semper, although clearly Wright's conception of built form as a petrified fabric writ large, most evident in his textile block houses of the 20s, derives directly from the cultural priority that Semper gave to textile production and to the knot as the primordial tectonic unit. It is arguable that Kahn was as much influenced by Wright as by the Franco-American Beaux-Arts line, stemming from Viollet-le-Duc and the Ecole des Beaux Arts. This particular genealogy enables us to recognise the links tying Kahn's Richards' Laboratories of 1959 back to Wright's Larkin Building. In each instance there is a similar 'tartan', textile-like preoccupation with dividing the enclosed volume and its various appointments into *servant* and *served* spaces. In addition to this there is a very similar concern for the *expressive rendering of mechanical services* as though they were of the same hierarchic importance as the structural frame. Thus the monumental brick ventilation shafts of the Richards' Laboratories are anticipated, as it were, in the hollow, ducted, brick bastions that establish the four-square monumental corners of

the Larkin Building. However dematerialised there is a comparable discrimination between servant and served spaces in Norman Foster's Sainsbury centre of 1978, combined with a similar penchant for the expressive potential of mechanical services. And here again we encounter further proof that the *tectonic* in the 20th century cannot concern itself only with structural form.

Wright's highly tectonic approach and the influence of this on the later phases of the modern movement have been underestimated, for Wright is surely the primary influence behind such diverse European figures as Carlo Scarpa, Franco Albini, Leonardo Ricci, Gino Valle and Umberto Riva, to cite only the Italian Wrightian line. A similar Wrightian connection runs through Scandinavia and Spain, serving to connect such diverse figures as Jorn Utzon, Xavier Saenz de Oiza and most recently Rafael Moneo, who as it happens was a pupil of both.

Something has to be said of the crucial role played by the joint in the work of Scarpa and to note the syntactically tectonic nature of his architecture. This dimension has been brilliantly characterised by Marco Frascari in his essay on the mutual reciprocity of constructing' and 'construing':

> Technology is a strange word. It has always been difficult to define its semantic realm. The changes in meaning, at different times and in different places of the word 'technology' into its original components of *techne* and *logos,* it is possible to set up a mirror-like relationship between the *techne* of *logos* and the *logos* of *techne*. At the time of the Enlightenment the rhetorical *techne* of *logos* was replaced by the scientific *logos* of *techne*. However, in Scarpa's architecture this replacement did not take place. Technology is present with both the forms in a chiastic quality. Translating this chiastic presence into a language proper to architecture is like saying that there is no construction without a construing, and no construing without a construction.[7]

Elsewhere Frascari writes of the irreducible importance of the joint not only for the work of Scarpa but for all tectonic endeavours. Thus we read in a further essay entitled 'The Tell-Tale Detail':

> Architecture is an art because it is interested not only in the original need for shelter but also in putting together, spaces and materials, in the meaningful manner. This occurs through formal and actual joints. The joint, that is the fertile detail, is the place where both the construction and the construing of architecture takes place. Furthermore, it is useful to complete our understanding of this essential role of the joint as the place of the process of signification to recall that the meaning of the original Indo-European root of the word *art* is joint . . .[8]

If the work of Scarpa assumes paramount importance for stress on the joint, the seminal value of Utzon's contribution to the evolution of modern tectonic form resides in his reinterpretation of Semper's 'four elements'. This is particularly evident in all his 'pagoda/podium' pieces that invariably break down into the earthwork and the surrogate hearth embodied in the podium and into the roof and the textile-like infill to be found in the form of the 'pagoda', irrespective of whether this crowning roof element comprises a shell vault or a folded slab (cf the Sydney Opera House of 1973 and the Bagsvaerd Church of 1977). It says something for Moneo's apprenticeship under Utzon that a similar articulation of earthwork and roof is evident in his Roman archaeological museum completed in Merida, Spain in 1986.

As we have already indicated, the tectonic lies suspended between a series of opposites, above all between the *ontological* and the *representational*. However, other dialogical conditions are involved in the articulation of tectonic form, particularly the contrast between the culture of the heavy-*stereotomics,* and the culture of the light-*tectonics.* The first implies load-bearing masonry and tends towards the earth and opacity. The second implies the dematerialised a-frame and tends towards the sky and translucence. At one end of this scale we have Semper's earthwork reduced in primordial times, as Gregotti reminds us, to the marking of ground. At the other end we have the ethereal, dematerialised aspirations of Joseph Paxton's Crystal Palace, that which Le Corbusier once described as the victory of light over gravity. Since few works are absolutely the one thing or the other, it can be claimed that the poetics of construction arise, in part, out of the inflection and positionings of the tectonic object. Thus the earthwork extends itself upwards to become an arch or a vault or alternatively withdraws first to become the cross wall support for a simple light-weight span and then to become a podium, elevated from the earth, on which an entire framework takes its anchorage. Other contrasts serve to articulate this dialogical movement further such as *smooth* versus *rough,* at the level of material (cf Adrian Stokes) or *dark* versus *light* at the level of illumination.

Finally, something has to be said about the signification of the 'break' or the 'dis-joint' as opposed to the signification of the joint. I am alluding to that point at which things break against each other rather than connect; that significant fulcrum at which one system, surface or material abruptly ends to give way to another. Meaning may be thus encoded through the interplay between 'joint' and 'break' and in this regard rupture may have just as much meaning as connection. Such considerations sensitise the architecture to the semantic risks that attend all forms of articulation, ranging from the over-articulation of joints to the under-articulation of form.

Postscriptum: Tectonic Form and Critical Culture

As Sigfried Giedion was to remark in the introduction to his two-volume study, *The Eternal Present* (1962), among the deeper impulses of modern culture in the first half of this century was a 'transavantgardist' desire to return to the timelessness of a pre-historic past; to recover in a literal sense some dimension of an eternal present, lying outside the nightmare of history and beyond the processal compulsions of instrumental progress. This drive insinuates itself again today as a potential ground from which to resist the commodification of culture. Within architecture the tectonic suggests itself as a mythical category with which to acquire entry to an anti-processal world wherein the 'presencing' of things will once again facilitate the appearance and experience of men. Beyond the aporias of history and progress and outside the reactionary closures of Historicism and the Neo-Avant-Garden, lies the potential for a *marginal* counter-history. This is the primaeval history of the logos to which Vico addressed himself, in his *Nuova Scienza,* in an attempt to adduce the poetic logic of the institution. It is a mark of the radical nature of Vico's thought that he insisted that knowledge is not just the province of objective fact but also a consequence of the subjective, 'collective' elaboration of archetypal myth, that is to say, an assembly of those existential symbolic truths residing in the human experience. The critical myth of the tectonic joint points to just this timeless, time-bound moment, excised from the continuity of time.

Notes

1. Hans Sedlmayr, *Art in Crisis: The Lost Centre*, Hollis and Carter Spottiswoode, Ballantyne & Co., Ltd., New York and London, 1957, p. 164.
2. Clement Greenberg, 'Modernist Painting', 1965. Republished in *The New Art* edited by Gregory Battcock, Dalton Paperback, New York, 1966, pp. 101-102.
3. Giorgio Grassi, 'Avant-Garde and Continuity', *Oppositions* No: 21, Summer, 1980 IAUS & MIT Press, pp. 26-27.
4. Ignasi Sola Morales, 'Critical Discipline', *Oppositions* No: 23, Winter 1981, IAUS & MIT Press, pp. 148-150.
5. Vittorio Gregotti, 'Lecture at the New York Architectural League', *Section A,* Vol. 1, No 1, Feb/Mar, 1983, Montreal, Canada.
6. Marco Frascari, 'Technometry and the work of Carlo Scarpa and MarioRidolf,'Proceedings of the ACSA National conference on Techndoom, Washington 1987
7. Marco Frascari, 'The Tell-Tale Detail' *VIA No. 7*, University of Pennsylvania.
8. See Joseph Mali, 'Mythology and Counter-History: The New Critical Art of Vico and Joyce'.

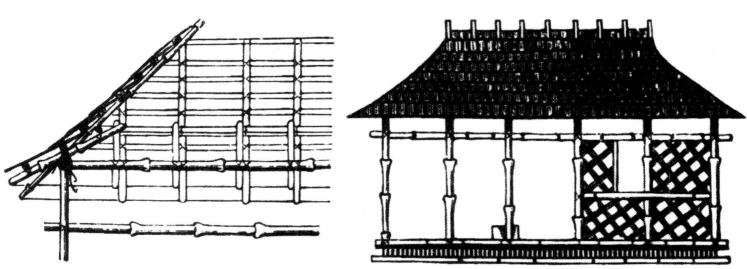

GOTTFRIED SEMPER, DRAWING OF CARRIBEAN HUT, EXHIBITED IN THE CARRIBEAN GREAT EXHIBITION OF 1851

CONRAD JAMESON

THE SUPER-MODERN DEFENCE: AN OPEN LETTER TO CHARLES JENCKS
An excerpt from Super-Modern Architecture

L TO *R*: COMPUTER RECONSTRUCTION OF THE BARCELONA PAVILION; GEORGES BRAQUE,*THE MANTELPIECE*, 1923

The central proposition of the super-modern defence is that an attack on modern architecture, whatever the variant, is an attack on all the modern arts. Why-pick-on-me may sound rather plaintive as a battle cry, yet delivered with a new-found confidence, it can be tellingly effective in doing the two things intended: raising the stakes about post-60s modern architecture even while drawing off fire.

You might think you are only attacking Le Corbusier and his descendants, run the super-modern defence. But you are in fact attacking Pablo Picasso and his descendants and Igor Stravinsky and his descendants and James Joyce and his descendants and Ezra Pound and his descendants and the New Critics and their descendants and Uncle Tom Cobbly and all their descendants who, after all, might criticise this modern work or that one yet will still salute Matthew Arnold's call to respect excellence wherever it may be found. And, let's face it, a lot of excellence can be found in the several modern arts and, lest you miss the point, in modern architecture, yes, even there.

As we behold modern architects standing shoulder to shoulder amid the multitude of practitioners in the several modern arts, all shaking their great beards, will not our hearts sink? And even if we are not smitten by fear will we not be smitten by filial piety as we observe that their beards are white and hoary with intellectual respectability? Could we be taking on not just the modern arts but, as art critic Clement Greenberg once observed, the artistic achievement of the 20th century?

Now I call the defence super-modern because, while latent from the beginnings of modern architecture, it only comes to the fore in the current division between post-moderns and late-moderns – and for reasons I must postpone, the term 'super-modern' fits them both. This late emergence is understandable.

Until recent years, modern architects kept their distance from the other modern arts in insisting that they should do their own stately thing – even when they didn't. Le Corbusier divided his time equally, he claimed, between architecture and painting. But he kept the halves apart. It just wouldn't do to be seen taking the sober thoughts of modern architects from, say, madcap modern painters who, tumbled from one unstable art movement to the next and fell out in between like pantomine clowns.

But as the other modern arts became more popular and modern architecture became less so the views of modern architects began to change. Like Richard II, they wondered whether their respective fortunes were not tied together like the buckets of a well, the other man's bucket dancing ever in the air, as Richard would have it, their own bucket down and full of tears. The idea could hardly fail to hit home that modern architects could pull themselves up in popularity – even if it meant pulling the other arts down, well, just a little and only for a while . . .

With so strong a common interest, all pulled together. But some pulled harder than others. One such was Charles Jencks, the leading spokesman for post-modern architecture and, as it happens, an old sparring partner whose views I have watched develop over the years.

Jencks had special reasons for bringing architecture into line with the other modern arts. For one, he needed instant intellectual re-inforcements, partly to help beat up the old modern architecture, partly to help get a new post-modern architecture on its feet. Where better to turn than to modernist literary critics, both American and French, who are not only known to be ferocious warriors in their own right but possess high-powered theories that, while out of kilter with early and late modern architecture, are remarkably apt for post-modern design? You have heard of heart and kidney transplants. Here is more daring surgery still: the transplant of a brain. Not since Frankenstein have we seen such a marriage: the mind of one activity inside the body of another.

For two, Jencks needed a PR campaign to show that post-modern architecture is a major event. What better PR than to demonstrate that Post-Modernism is a wide-spread movement in the arts, nay, a revolution, as Jencks himself claims, that has 'cut across film, music, dance, religion, politics, fashion and nearly every activity of contemporary life'?

The critic can't help but sigh. Here we go once more with the same old appeal to the *Zeitgeist* that brought in the old modern architecture and with the same old over-bearing demand to lie down and be run over by the juggernaut of history. And here we go once more with the same old snigger that if you don't comply with the *Zeitgeist* you are demonstrating not so much a disagreement but bad faith. But the critic also can't help take alarm. If the PR campaign worked the last time round, why should it not work again? And if it could work again, what are we going to do about it?

We can't just walk away from the super-modern defence. There is in fact a broad-scale post-modern movement and, crazily enough, it does embrace fields as diverse as fashion and religion. And there are in fact common practices and ideas in the several post-modern arts, so common in fact that post-modern painting and post-modern architecture are now twin disciplines that Jencks in his recent writings quite reasonably treats as one. And it is in fact hypocritical to attack one modern art without attacking the others – not to say painful and confusing as our hypocrisy turns the arts into a lawless country where a crime one day becomes acceptable behaviour the next.

On the other hand we can't do battle with the super-modern defence. That would be to walk into a trap. We could be biting off more than we can chew in taking on the several modern arts – assuming we had the appetite in the first place or, for that matter, any appetite left over to take on architecture after so jaw-breaking a mastication.

Or could we be exaggerating the strength of the super-modern defence? Even more importantly, could we be failing to see that it opens up just the opportunity we have been looking for ?

Dear Charlie,

It must be as curious to you as it is to me that we should both have started out throwing grenades at modern architecture yet ended up on opposite sides of the barricades. Each of us wrote a critique of campus architecture, one of the University of Essex, the other of the Mies van der Rohe's Illinois Institute of Technology. Both of us made the same point: a place of learning had been made to look like a place of work – an out-of-town office complex in the first instance and a factory park in the second. Even in spite of themselves such designs conveyed, we argued, the very idea that architects and educators alike were trying to keep secret: that the modern campus is only a production line – with the student coming out of it considered less a person than a thing. Stones speak, said the Romans. And so, we argued, do concrete and steel. I wrote the first critique. You wrote the second. That is, if I remember correctly. It could have been the other way around.

Not that it would have mattered. We had long realised that mine and thine were so confused we dare not give the other a compliment for fear of scratching his own back. Friends, colleagues, fellow American ex-patriots in London, alumni of the same university (and even the same courses in English literature), we were a standing caution against co-workers living in each other's pockets. It made me nervous to realise that even our initials are identical. Did I write your manuscripts? Did you write mine?

It took us years to realise that similar critiques led to dissimilar conclusions – plus years more to admit that, whatever the cause of the other's aberration, the condition itself was long term and degenerative. All we could then do is flap about confused and abashed, agreeing to disagree, yet never really figuring out why. But if the sources of our disagreement even now leave us scratching our heads, there is still a question that can be retrieved from the muddle, a question, as it happens, that could be of value and interest to those on my side of the barricades who must do battle against the super-modern defence: why did it take us so long to discover that we disagreed at all? Something must have clouded our minds. That something, I suggest, could be clouding other minds as well.

You grew up inside the architectural establishment as an architect and architectural historian. From the beginning you were, like other members of the architectural establishment, a paid-up member of the modern movement – and no less loyal, of course, because critical of your colleagues. By contrast I was an outsider coming into architecture – in my case from applied social research – and was not just hostile to modern architecture from the start but hostile in the manner of someone outside the tribe. Surely we should have seen quickly enough that in time we would disagree – and the more surely as I was soon arguing from my own research that the fault in modern architecture lay not in this building design or that one but in the very language of modern architecture itself. The popular rejection of modern buildings, I argued, arises not because people are slow or dim-witted or philistine, as modern architects would have us believe, but for the same reason that Hungarian school children have trouble learning Russian: because the language itself is alien and imposed.

To be fair, I should admit that at the time you had no hint of my later apostacy – not surprisingly, as at the time I had no hint of it myself. I had taken off a year to investigate social research techniques that could be applied to architecture. If only research could be more sensitive in gaging user reactions, I told myself, the language of modern architecture could be smoothed of its abrasiveness. You might have thought that at the end of my study I would have concluded that, as the language of modern architecture was the root problem, modern architecture itself must be replaced. But that is not at all what I concluded. What I actually concluded was only that architects and social scientists should get together in a new partnership of skills. If the language of modern architecture was insensitive, then the answer was simple: make it more sensitive by calling in social scientists to find out what kind of designs people liked and understood. In a word, I assumed reform rather than counter-revolution in taking the popular party line of the architectural establishment itself: the answer to bad modern architecture is simply better modern architecture.

But then again, to be fair, what other party line could either of us have expected? If modern architecture is bad, that didn't make its alternative any better. For what was the alternative to modern architecture but thatched cottage nostalgia or Georgian pastiche or a pontifical classical architecture that would look authoritarian enough on a police headquarters but downright ridiculous on a nuclear power station? Admittedly, modern architecture raises hostility and often well deserved. But let's keep things in perspective. When did any new architecture fail to raise hostility? When did any new art find instant acceptance? And who (let us not forget it!) were the great enemies of modern architecture but the Nazis and, for that matter, who (let us not forget this either!) were the great supporters of a traditionalist revival but the Nazis as well? And, even if politics are put aside, isn't massive hostility to modern architecture at bottom a psychological resistance to a new way of seeing and feeling that breaks through the over-grown cliches of the past, a resistance that conceals only our regressive desire to go backwards in time to the comforts and security of an imaginary past? But we can't go back to our old Kentucky home! We have crossed the river into the present over a bridge now blown away! We have said goodbye just in growing up!

In retrospect my arguments at the time only strike me as wet-nosed and naive. All I can say in defence is that at the time I spoke as you did and as did others of the same background. But then we were children of the modern movement. We had grown up in the house of modern architecture. It was the only house we knew. And just as we knew only the house of modern architecture, so we knew only the terraces of similar houses where lived the other modern arts. Here was our neighbourhood and here was our town. We could run in and out of doors between one house and another, now visiting modern music, now modern painting, now modern ballet, yet always sure of a welcome – and equally sure we liked and understood our neighbours even in their not infrequent quarrels. What values and thoughts we shared with our neighbours would be hard to say. These were the unself-conscious days before the super-modern defence when you didn't have to give whys and wherefores. It was enough to know where in heart and mind you belonged.

But if some bold philistine had even then challenged us to reveal the common ground of our wider loyalties we could have hit back swiftly. There is a single modern movement, we would have said, to which all the modern arts belong in sharing the same philosophy and often even the same techniques. What did modern architecture share with modern painting? But could you not see it! The same flat planes you found in Picasso's Cubist paintings you found again in Mies van der Rohe's Barcelona Pavilion. What did modern architecture share with modern music? But could you not hear it! The same exciting dissonance you found in Stravinsky's *Rites of Spring* you found again in Le Corbusier's Villa Savoye where a ramp and corkscrew stair sit harshly side by side. Even if we were to leap forward to the end of the 70s there would have been no less a sense of union with the other arts when you yourself began to preach a post-modern architecture studded with historical quotations. What did modern architecture – or post-modern architecture, if you wish – share with modern poetry? But could you not read it! The same collage of quotations you found in Ezra Pound's *Cantos* or T S Eliot's *The Wasteland* you found again in Philip Johnson's skyscraper for AT&T.

As a critic of modern architecture, I could of course have been caught out even then for inconsistency. If I thought the language of modern architecture so abrasive, why wasn't I also hard on what was presumably the equally abrasive language of Cubist painting? But there was an easy answer – and all of us used it. The geography of the modern arts, we rebutted, had to be taken into account. The houses of the other arts ran down a private lane. Only architecture was on a visible corner of a busy main street. A painting you may not look at, a composition you may not listen to, a poem you may not read. But architecture is willy nilly the art you foist upon your neighbour, the literal *res publica* that defines our common life. But of course architecture is the exception! And of course different rules apply!

At any rate that is what you and I told each other at the time.

And of course – or so I am tempted to add with the gift of hindsight – what we told each other was a lie. Never mind whether the modern arts are all of a piece. The fact remains that *we* are all of a piece. We cannot denounce a Cubist language in a modern building on a Monday only to admire the same Cubist language in a modern painting on a Tuesday. Even if we could master the logical inconsistency, we could never master the inner confusion. The lie may be admittedly convenient. But all it does in the end is turn counter-insurgents against modern architecture into self-crippled neurotics. No more could Abraham bring down his knife against Isaac than could I or other critics bring down our knife against modern architecture. A voice always came to us at the last moment, a voice that told us that modern architecture is no different than the other modern arts, our modern arts, the modern arts we grew up with, the modern arts we love.

Now if we trace back our secret loyalties, I submit, we shall find them tied not to this art or that one but to a linguistic equivalent of an Oedipal knot: the mother tongue that, picked up early on with finger painting at school, gets us thinking about the arts in a modernist sort of way – whether we care for the thinking or not. We don't speak this modernist language. A modernist language speaks us.

A painful incident. You will see what I mean. Tricia and I were sitting in the lobby of a hotel in Dubrovnik when a man introduced himself, as an official from the American Embassy in Belgrade. The Merce Cunningham dance troupe was performing that evening. Could he interest us in complimentary tickets? He then explained that the dance troupe was the American contribution to the Dubrovnik international festival of the arts and that we were people, he was sure, who would enjoy the performance. I got the message. Only the evening before, I explained, I heard a piano recital at the Rector's Palace by a contributor from the Eastern block, a Polish Amazon of a pianist who had thumped out Chopin so loudly I expected that by way of encore she would lift the piano over her head. If that was what international cultural competitions were about, I told the embassy official, warming to my theme . . . but it was too late. Tricia tucked the tickets in her purse. After a brandy, she told him, my husband will see things differently. He left puzzled but pleased.

Tricia was of course right. After a brandy, I was happy as a sand-boy, sitting in an open-air theatre overlooking the sea and taking pleasure in an avant-garde dance troupe that was hell-bent, or so it seemed to me, on giving no pleasure at all. But then its indifference to my pleasure didn't itself displease as I had more than pleasure enough in finding the hidden sanity in what was otherwise avant-garde lunacy. It was like picking up a book in a language you had studied at school. It didn't matter what the book said. It was enough to realise that, even after years of neglect, you could still read it. In a traditional ballet, there is a *pas de deux*. In Cunningham's avant-garde ballet, there is a *pas à trois*, the third part taken by the wizened Merce Cunningham himself who carried a long stick. No sooner would the lovers start to dance than he would put his stick in their way. In a traditional ballet, the dancers wear tights. In Cunningham's avant-garde ballet the dancers wore thick warming-up socks and scarves. In a traditional ballet, the dancers leap about. In Cunningham's avant-garde ballet, the dancers only walk about.

I thought of Martha Graham and her ballet for Aaron Copland's *Appalachian Springs*, the pioneer work that had put American modern dance on the map. The wheel had gone full circle. At the beginning, modern dance was to have challenged the snobberies of classical ballet in forcing it to give up its élitist tutus and pirouettes for a new and accessible language of the people. Even the words of the American folk-tune in *Appalachian Springs* told you as much: 'It's a gift to be simple/ It's a gift to be free/It's a gift to come down/Where you ought to be.' Now with Cunningham the language of the people was in a Latin indecipherable to all but the few.

But I also thought of Sir John Summerson's essay about the language of Le Corbusier as a turning of convention upside down. In classical architecture the columns sit atop a podium. In the architecture of Le Corbusier, the podium sits atop the columns. In 19th-century town planning a huge park is placed inside the town. In the town planning of Le Corbusier, the town is put inside a huge park. You could accuse the new language of perversity. But you could also accuse its detractors of philistinism. As with any language, you have to make the effort to get use to it. But once learned you can then discover its expressive potential. And was not the language of Merce Cunningham indeed expressive? Was there not something quite apt, something more like our real lives in a *pas de deux* that doesn't take place, in the stick that gets in the way? And wasn't there something apt even in the anti-convention of ending a scene with a pirouette, quite as if to say that we can now stop responding as we are back to the everyday world of cliche?

At any rate such were my thoughts when it began to drizzle. Most of the audience left. We remained among a handful of die-hards half-hidden under our coats.

The next day we were again sitting in the hotel lobby and were again approached, this time by the hotel manager and two of his colleagues. He plainly had something to say. I see you stayed on at the ballet, he started in. Yes, I replied, it was a pity that so many people had to leave because of the rain. Because of the rain! he exclaimed. My remark must have been astonishing as, still speaking in English, he turned to his colleagues and repeated it. They stood so still I could only wonder what would happen next. Would 'because of the rain' turn into a song? Would the three men break into a dance routine? No such luck. Do you think the people of Dubrovnik, he cried, will be insulted? Do you think that we need your country's charity? Do you think that just because you give something away you can empty out your pig styes?

You didn't like the performance? I ventured lamely. That was a mistake. Didn't like the performance! he exclaimed, once again repeating the words to his colleagues. I mean it would be better, I said, trying desperately again, if America had sent something more traditional like *Swan Lake*. That was a bigger mistake. It would be better, he said slowly as if he suddenly realised I was mentally ill, if your country didn't dump pigswill on our heads! Tricia butted in. We had to see for ourselves, she said. Her voice rose like the bugles of a calvary troop just arriving over the hill. Disgraceful! she said, shaking her head. Disgraceful! I echoed. Someone should write the American ambassador, she added. And I shall! I chimed in. Will you? asked the hotel manager. Yes of course! I exclaimed. At which point he and his colleagues shook us cordially by the hand. A few minutes later the hotel manager came back and handed me a piece of paper with an address on it. I know you and your wife wanted a room with a sea view, he said. I have just the room up the road. It's in the flat of my mother.

Psychoanalyse the matter as you wish. I meant to write the ambassador. I just forgot. Or maybe I couldn't get my thoughts together after the electric jolts of the occasion. Whatever the explanation, I was sure that I had been rattled enough to lapse into the posturing attitudes of my class – and by class I don't mean U and non-U in the old Nancy Mitford sense of the term but the newer snobberies of the university educated that Britons rather euphemistically call the chattering classes. As members of the chattering classes you and I don't have to like this modern work or that one. But you do have to know how to read a modern work, to understand its Latin. Indeed the *aficionado* is supposed to understand it so well that he doesn't even think about

translation – always a vulgar and distasteful thing in the modern arts – but can take in and absorb the work as he might take in and absorb sunshine or air. Well or badly Tricia and I took in enough. It was a sign of our class membership to do so – our anti-snob snobberies of the more conventional kind notwithstanding.

But the taking in and absorbing of avant-garde art could also be a sign of something else: habits of mind so engrained that, even should we be traitors to the chattering classes, the intellectual style and manner would remain. If I thought the ballet was going to upset the audience (and in the wrong sort of way) I would have opposed it. But that wouldn't be the same as saying that I myself didn't like it. I did like it and for reasons that went far deeper than could be explained by class loyalty: a ballet with a flatfooted *pas à trois* made sense to me and not just as an idea or theme but as a way of making art.

There was nothing wrong with the old bourgeois art of classical ballet, I told myself, provided of course you knew it was old and bourgeois. What would be wrong, and profoundly so, would be to think that the old art could take the place of the new. Our own time must be served – and with an art of its own as well. Or so as a child of the modern movement I thought.

But suppose for a moment we put, not me on the couch, but the modernist habits of mind that I shared with you and others of our class. Take the opposition I myself assumed: *Swan Lake* versus Merce Cunningham. What a perfect gem of modernist propaganda I had taken in and regurgitated onto the lap of the unsuspecting hotel manager! On the one hand was the fossilised and sentimental. On the other was the up-to-date and challenging. That was the clear choice between the two types of ballet, the one traditional, the other modern. But suppose we change the terms of the opposition. Let's not talk about tutus versus warming-up socks. Let's not even talk of classical versus modern. Let's talk instead about a much simpler opposition: telling a story and not telling a story.

Observe: we now see a different picture – and a picture that is far more accurate! I had got it wrong about *Swan Lake* in seeing it as hopelessly marooned in the past. *Swan Lake* tells a story. But so does Stravinsky's *Rites of Spring* and Martha Graham's *Appalachian Springs*. *Swan Lake* belongs in fact to an evolving tradition of story-telling in ballet, a rather jerky and disrupted tradition, to be sure, as its language has changed rapidly with the stories it has to tell. But then traditionalists are likely to take a lenient view of what is or isn't traditional in an art that only goes back to the beginnings of the last century.

But I had also got it wrong about Merce Cunningham in seeing his *pas à trois* as another and more up-to-date type of story. It was not. I should have gathered as much from the music – or rather the non-music as what passed for music was an atonal blowing on a conch. The music for traditional story-telling ballet – modern or classical, as the case may be – has to be tonal, has to come back to the tonic, otherwise the story wouldn't have a beginning and an end. It was just this beginning and an end that Cunningham's ballet lacked. How blind of me not to notice! But I also should have guessed from Cunningham's anti-convention conventions: if the opposite of leaping is walking, then the opposite of story-telling is not story-telling. The stick doesn't just interrupt the lovers. It interrupts the story itself.

We can now isolate a modernist habit of mind so engrained it had all but pushed me, willy-nilly, into a defence of avant-garde ballet. Cunningham was practising an art of ambiguity – what you and post-moderns would nowadays call an art of multivalence – in which stories (along with meanings and morals) are made purposely indecipherable. Long may he do so – just as long, that is, that no one tells us that the hotel manager or anyone else is a fool or philistine in rejecting the huge and terrible choice between the dead art of the past and the live art of the present. That choice is simply modernist propaganda. I might write the American ambassador after all!

But now take the swear words which I instinctively hurled at traditionalist alternatives to modern architecture: 'sentimental', 'pastiche', 'a nostalgic going back'. You can't help notice that these modernist swear words are all but tautologies of a single idea: fake. I might have thought that I was saying different and devastating things about traditionalist architecture but in fact I could have saved myself time and energy by repeating only one. By the same token, the good things I assumed about modern design were a constant repetition of the antonymn to fake: authentic. Just think of all the moral passion I put into such lovely words as 'honest', 'original' (in the sense of going back to origins), 'radical' (again in the sense of going back to roots), 'uncompromising', 'of our time'. The single word 'authentic' could have taken their place! Indeed I could have spared myself even the trouble of thinking about traditional and modern designs as, sight unseen, I would know what to think by pressing a mental button and allowing the toy soldiers marked 'authentic' to shoot down the toy soldiers marked 'fake'. Here is a traditional design. It will be sentimental, pastiche, a nostalgic going back.

perhaps one example might suffice.

By a modernist way of thinking, a classical revival can mean only a return to the pompous and pontifical. Admittedly, a classical revival could indeed mean just that. Certainly there is nothing to stop us going back to the style of the Paris Opera House or indeed of Albert Speer. But why couldn't a classical revival go back more sensibly to, say, Thomas Jefferson's University of Virginia and in just the way that Jefferson himself went back: by picking and choosing among classical precedents? In the event Jefferson found the classical precedent for his great library, the Roman Pantheon of the second century AD, too pompous and pontifical by half – indeed by exactly half, it would seem, as he adapted the precedent of the Pantheon by literally halving its size. Jefferson also more than halved the impact of the materials. The Pantheon is a temple of stone. But the library is only a temple in small part as the building is in fair-faced brick. Only the classical ornament is an imitation of stone and a down-played imitation at that of plain white paint.

Here could be the clue to the classical design of the police headquarters: finding not only the right precedent but adapting the precedent to the occasion – adjusting its decorum, as

L TO *R*: HASSAN FATHY, THE INTERNATIONAL MOVEMENT IN VERNACULAR ARCHITECTURE; UNIVERSITY OF ESSEX

Here is a modern design. You can be sure it will be honest, original, radical, uncompromising and of our time.

The only problem with the modernist opposition, fake/authentic, is that its application is so arbitrary as to defeat its own purpose. Is the latest glass shoe-box in the modern manner still the authentic way of saying 'factory' in our own time – even if we can forget that the first glass shoe-box (appropriately enough for a shoe manufacturer) was designed by Walter Gropius in 1911? And if a glass shoe-box is still the authentic way of saying 'factory' why in New England is it less authentic to say 'house' with white clapboard and dark shutters and a porch? Or is the American clapboard house to be ruled out as inauthentic because it happens to be older than a glass shoe-box and comes with architectural plans you can still buy off the peg?

But I mustn't go on – not at least for the moment. Enough to say that in each and every case whether it is the definition of Georgian or the facts about a traditionalist revival in Hitler's Germany or even the definition of authenticity itself – we shall find either a gross abuse of the historical facts or an equally gross distortion of the language itself that forever re-routes the argument so that it comes to a modernist conclusion. For now

classicists would say, so as to strike the right moral balance between the modest and the grand. And here too could be the clue to the nuclear power station. The Victorians thought that the civic order extended to water towers and dressed them accordingly. That was their privilege. Ours is to judge whether a nuclear power station is inside or outside the civic order – and, if inside at all, to what degree. The pure temple in civic architecture, remember, is a rarity. The more usual civic design borrows from the classical vocabulary only in small part with the amount borrowed depending on what we think about the decorum of the building itself. I say 'we' advisedly because decorum is always a moral rather than an aesthetic question and its answer demands a public laying on of hands. Or could this public laying on of hands be the real prejudice behind the modernist manner of assuming that a classical revival equates only with the pompous and pontifical: such a revival would mean a shift to lay power and a clipping of the modern architect's privileges and powers?

If, for the sake of argument, we can assume that other modernist ways of thinking show the same kind of prejudice, we can go back to the question I started with: why we had so much difficulty even admitting we disagreed. With the gift of hindsight the answer is only too obvious: we couldn't understand our disagreements because underneath our arguments were miles and miles of shared modernist assumptions anchored in the very language we speak. And that in a nutshell has been the problem, I suggest, not just for me but for the masses of lay conservationists on my side of the barricades.

We could easily enforce our will by turning from defence to attack. Yet we never get around to it as we are so brain-washed by modernist propaganda we have come to see even our own traditionalist alternatives in a blur, sometimes literally so . . .

Consider the white hope of a traditional revival in the 70s: the experiments of the Egyptian architect-philosopher, Hassan Fathy, to bring back vernacular housing of mud and straw to the village of Gourna near Luxor – even though the self-build techniques had lapsed so long Fathy had to import workmen from Nubia who could still remember the old ways of building. And what splendid old ways of building they proved to be! For here it was not just speed and low cost and environmental suitability that made a laughing stock of the concrete rabbit hutches of modern architects. Here was breath-taking beauty in domed houses with sun screens and courtyards and boldly

former editor of *Country Life* and a director of Save, Britain's most powerful conservationist lobby. He was talking about the post-modern Observer Building of 1987 hardly a stone's throw across the Thames from Sir Christopher Wren's Chelsea Hospital yet a building so vulgar in its mock-classical, Disneyland style you had trouble yourself in acknowledging that it is a post-modern building at all. Yet Binney's opinion was quickly seconded by another self-confessed traditionalist, columnist Simon Jenkins, deputy director of English Heritage, the official government body charged with protecting Britain's historic buildings. Jenkins' reaction was in fact predictable. Not long before he had attacked Prince Charles for attacking modern architects. Didn't the Prince realise, asked Jenkins, that with the advent of post-modern design 'the Great Mistake is over'?

A year later came a re-run of a major public inquiry for the same sensitive site near the Bank of England that had thrown out the posthumous design by Mies van der Rohe. But this time the contender wasn't one of your glass-wrapped 'dumb boxes', as you aptly call them, but a design by Britain's foremost post-modern architect, James Stirling. Prince Charles was hostile but, unaccountably, didn't lobby against it, possibly because one of

L TO R: THOMAS JEFFERSON, UNIVERSITY OF VIRGINIA; ROMAN PANTHEON

patterned doors. Britain picked up the idea of a vernacular revival early on in the counter-revolutionary *Essex Design Guide* of 1973 that showed builders that they could not only build at low cost in the indigenous East Anglia style of dark woods and brick but that these vernacular-style houses would actually sell better than contemporary style alternatives.

But what happened to the vernacular revival itself? Even by the late 70s it turned into a blur. A revival vernacular in Britain became anything in brick with slate-clad dormer windows. A revival of vernacular on the Greek islands became anything painted white with a flat roof. A revival of vernacular in Provence became anything painted pink with a sloping roof of tiles. The counter-revolution soon lost its interest in rethinking materials and costs and uses and forms. So desperate was the counter-revolutionary need – yet so tongue-tied was the expression of the need itself by modernist habits of mind – any rough semblance of vernacular would do.

The same blurring – and for the same reasons – was equally evident in traditionalist reactions to a new modern architecture that claimed to be reformed. 'The greatest building since the war!' exclaimed self-confessed traditionalist Marcus Binney, a

his closest advisors, *New Statesman* critic Jules Lubbock, had only recently written a defence of Stirling's new museum in Stuttgart. The traditionalist case was left largely in the hands of Save and English Heritage which, instead of attacking the Stirling design head-on, decided to defend instead the building that would have to be torn down to make way for it, an endearing piece of classical Edwardiana but one which even the most ardent conservationists could still rank no better than second-rate.

In the meantime the post-moderns – you among them – had gone on the offensive. Here is Contextural design, the post-moderns pleaded, in pointing out that the stone cladding and roof-line would match with their neighbours – and this despite the fact that the design boasts pink stone, an Egyptian trapezoid entrance fit for *Aida*, a giant Moorish style key-hole arch, a turret facing the Bank of England in the manner of a ship's forecastle and, lest any one miss the show-stopping point, undulating glass walls that all but wiggle for attention! The thumbs-up of the government inspector came as no surprise. The Stirling design, concluded the baffled official, is 'just possibly a master-piece.'

It isn't difficult to see what has happened is a will to believe –

or, perhaps more accurately, a will to forget. The Great Mistake, after all, wasn't just the mistake of modern architects. It was the collective mistake of us all. Hence the appeal of a philosophy of *meno male*, as worldly Italians would call it, by which we are asked to be grateful for suffering less.

After all, these laymen reassure us, modern architects are no longer designing vandal-ridden, high-rise public housing. Nor are they ganging up with bureaucrats or developers to flatten whole streets and neighbourhoods under the hideous title of urban renewal. What they are doing (or at any rate what postmoderns are doing, so a Save or English Heritage would tell us) is at least trying to hold on to tradition, trying to carry forward a rememberance of the vernacular, trying to revive something of the classical past, trying to fit in to the neighbourhood – and that is more than can be said for modern architects heretofore. No doubt a bit of literary silliness gets mixed in with the post-modern craze of quotation. But when you get down to it, what does it matter provided the new modern architecture isn't as boring as the old?

Yesterday the New York skyscraper wore the head-dress of a gothic spire. The day after that it slicked back its hair in the Chrysler building to look like the futuristic *bouffant* of a Radio City Rockette. The day after that it went in for a tabletop crew-cut. And the day after that it plumbed for Philip Johnson's jazzy classical pediment. It is arguable of course that the new head-dress is Greek in more ways than one. Certainly there is no evidence that the hubris of corporate power is any less intact. But let's be fair. Isn't the new style of modern architecture at least marginally better than the dumb boxes of yesterday?

Now when I hear such arguments from my fellow citizen-soldiers I would despair were I not aware that there is at least an outside chance of our being spared defeat in spite of ourselves by a knockabout comedy of events. I refer to the advent of the super-modern defence which finds the modernist opposition racing into battle, stepping on a rake and bopping itself on the head. You will tell me that at the very sound of its war-like music we should shudder and quake. But I will tell you that such sounds gladden our hearts and that even the sight of such a lame, rag-taggle army clanking into battle is enough to make us throw our hats in the air!

For surely the super-modern defence is the perfect adversary we have been waiting for, the enemy that reminds us of our duties, forces us to pull our socks up yet – not at all in the way that the super-modern defence intends! – neither distracts our minds nor depletes our energies. As a foil to our own sleepy assumptions, the super-modern defence couldn't be more solicitous of our needs.

First it bugles us awake in reminding us that the enemy is not just modern architecture but the several modern arts – and not just the several modern arts but a modernist way of thinking that at once undercuts and embraces them all. Our trouble all along has been our over-confidence in thinking that, with popular support behind us, we can if we so wish beard modern architecture and throw it over our shoulder. Now that we see that there are a number of beards to pull – not to mention a number of fifth columnists insinuated into our own ranks we are forced on the alert. *Aux armes*! cries the super-modern defence. At last we rub our eyes! *Aux armes* it will be!

And no sooner does the super-modern defence wake us up than, with equal kindness, it replaces overconfidence with the real confidence that all along we have secretly lacked. For what better way to do so than to reveal that the modernist opposition is no longer the terrible enemy that we feared. It is tempting to think that there is a single modern movement more or less the same over time. But that isn't the case – and no one has done more than you to call attention to the fact. For by putting 'post'

in front of a new movement in the arts you have inadvertently planted a warning flag to tell us that something immense has happened, that the whole modern movement has undergone a sea change that has transformed it out of all recognition.

In succeeding chapters, we shall see that we are dealing with a fundamentalist movement that makes the several modern arts *more* modern – or what I shall call super-modern. Of this purification there is no doubt. There is a cleaning out of traditionalist elements of just the kind I had stumbled across in Cunningham but had failed to notice – not least, I should add, because you and others had yet to signal that, along with the other arts, ballet was entering a fundamentalist, super-modern phase in which it purges itself of the traditionalist past. But we shall also see that we are dealing with a far weaker movement, of that there can be no doubt either.

No wonder the white-bearded leaders of the modern movement seemed so venerable and august! Look more closely. They are already dead! Nor have the super-modern arts agreed on leaders to replace them. And no wonder the new army of modernists make such a din! Listen more closely. It is neither conversation nor argument that we hear nor the shouts of war. What we hear is Babel! Quick-changing movements and styles we have known before. But here are convulsions of a different kind: a massive falling out among practitioners of the same art who share neither a movement nor a style. In the super-modern arts of the post-60s, you can not even imagine a Picasso and Braque working together to develop their joint ideas about Cubist painting. Each and every super-modern artist is expected to invent his own style – with the number of new styles now only practically limited by the number of famous practitioners that editors of arts magazines can remember. Even this practical criterion is set on its ear by zealots who insist that, in the pious name of authenticity and anti-cliche, a true aesthetic experience is singular and unrepeatable. Ergo, a new style must be invented from one work of art to the next.

And, as if the falling out of Babel were not enough to unman the super-modernists, they are debilitated still further by an epidemic of what might be called Moral Aids: what looks like a slow and slovenly moral response turns out to be a dangerous disability to throw off corruption. On first confronting the super-modern art of the post-60s, it is easy to make the same mistake I made myself in thinking that, as Cunningham is telling a different story, he is trafficking only in different if more complicated morals and meanings. In truth Cunningham is quite typical of the super-modern arts in telling rather a non-story that carries only anti-morals and anti-meanings – and with complexity itself exploited to evade not just moral commitment but any sort of moral judgement whatsoever.

At bottom you find in the post-60s super-modern arts only an old-fashioned aesthetic of art-for-art's sake. But here is no longer an Oscar Wilde preaching the limp-wristed beauty of useless things or a Walter Pater hungering for art as a delicate soul-food for nourishing the 'highest quality to your moments as they pass.' Here is art-for-art's-sake in the hands of zealots who, in their lust for purification, treat morals and meanings as intrusions to be searched out and destroyed – 'deconstructed', in the fashionable phrase. Be it for a new work or a classic, the business of the super-modern critic is to take the text and tear its morals and meanings apart – including of course those shared morals and meanings we call our common traditions – and show that they are only a multiplicity of contradictions at odds even with the intention of the artist himself, that is, if the artist were so foolish as to intend morals and meanings in the first place.

Now we shall find just such super-modern ideas in modern architecture even during the 60s. Yet even through the early 70s modern architecture remains remarkably immune, partly no doubt because of its special needs for moral respectability, but more because critics who guarded the gate were themselves hostile. One particular critic comes to mind of unusual astuteness who even by 1973 had carefully studied the super-modern ideas that even then were drifting in from the other arts. As a police dog sniffs out drugs, so this astute critic sniffed out moral danger.

The paradigm for these new super-modern ideas, he reasoned, was Andy Warhol's famous painting of a Campbell soup can. At first glance, you could think that here was only a light-hearted send-up – and in a traditionalist manner that at long last brought back representation in art. For what do we see but a mass-produced soup can painted as if it were a religious icon? But a closer inspection showed a quite different idea: the foiling and incapacitation of a moral response. For here was not a painting of a mass-produced object. Here was a painting of a photograph of a mass-produced object, quite as if the artist were trying to make it impossible to say whether the mass-produced soup can should be valued, revalued or devalued – or all three in turn.

An amusing idea, argued this critic, yet transferred to the public art of architecture it could only alarm. An architecture that only played with morality, he reasoned, would licence just the kind of thing you found in Philip Johnson's church in New Harmony, Indiana: monumental gates festooned with heavy wreaths of a kind last seen in the architecture of the Third Reich. An accident? Or was Johnson not bringing back a Third Reich imagery he had so admired before the war? But then Johnson was even then exploiting the same ideal of moral ambiguity in art that had created Warhol's soup can. Here was a new twist to the Biblical injunction of judge not so you be not judged. Judge not because super-modern art is so ambiguous you cannot judge at all.

This same astute critic also saw that an architecture of moral ambiguity was quintessentially egotistical in calling attention to the artist himself. For what did this new aesthetic argue but that the artist was beyond the law, not because he asserted a law of his own, but because he could find (or so he alleged) no law to assert. Again an amusing idea, argued this critic, yet transferred to the public art of architecture the joke spelled something ominous: that the very public domain that architecture is meant to serve would in time erode and disappear. It could not be otherwise. A public domain depends not just on a spoken public morality but on a hidden private restraint – including the restraint of the individual architect. But it was just such restraint that an architecture of moral ambiguity would lack in calling attention to itself and in making the architect notorious if only for refusing to accept that the public must ratify his moral views.

This astute critic wanted a name for a new and dangerous form of modern architecture that was just then making headway, a name that would stick in the mind yet describe the new modern architecture for what it is. He borrowed the label from Susan Sontag but the choice was no less brilliant for that. Sorry to remind you. You called it Camp.

Five years later you changed the name 'Camp' by deed poll. You now called it Post-Modern Architecture. Once this architecture bore your own storm warnings. Now this same architecture was to become a reformist cause that would, as you later prophesied, 'slow if not halt the destruction of our cities.'

What had happened to explain the *volte face*? The answer, I suggest, is that nothing happened. You simply stayed inside the modern movement and epic changes in the modern movement itself did the rest. Why did you stay? The question is inevitable yet unfair. You stayed for the same reasons that I eventually left; which is to say, for reasons that are ultimately unfathomable. But if the cause of your staying is unknown, the effect of your staying was only too predictable. You were forced into a contradiction. In the one breath you condemned the moral ambiguity of Warhol's portrait of a soup can. In another you extolled complexity and contradiction that conveniently did away with the need for moral judgement. Can even you be surprised that in time you settled down to a comforting have-your-cake-and-eat-it philosophy whereby you could pick and choose amonst the other modern arts so as to keep modern architecture free from contagion – and do so even while staying in with the other modern arts for purposes of public relations?

It is at this point that the super-modern defence does one last service – and for those of us on my side of the barricades it is the kindest of all: remind us that, just as there was once a single modern movement, there is now a single super-modern movement that embraces all the arts – including of course the new modern architecture. It is as if, in standing together, the several super-modern arts frame a silhouette that defines irrefutability a true picture of the new architecture. Where the new modern architecture fits this silhouette we shall discover its true soul and self. But where it fails to fit, we shall find only public relations and what Hegel would call 'false consciousness.'

Admittedly such allegations are still to be proved. But thanks once more to the super-modern defence we now know not only where to look for the evidence but the nature of the architectural beast. Only the spots have changed. The leopard is the same – but is now the more dangerous for its camouflage. For here is a second wave of modern architecture that, if more slow-moving than the first, is yet and more emphatically the old beast we know too well: more cocky, more contemptuous, more insistent on the architect's powers and prerogatives, more egomaniacal, more given to self-monuments, more willing as the henchman of corrupt and corrupting powers-that-be, more disruptive of our civic bonds, more disorienting in tearing apart our collective memories and beliefs, more socially divisive, more destructive of our neighbourhoods and cities, more, in a word, as it always was and still remains but, liquified and distilled into a new and potent purity, more modern and fundamentalist than ever before: lo, Super-Modern Architecture!

Will those on my side of the barricades, the instinctive enemies of modern architecture, take note of so strange and dangerous a transformation? It would be hard to say. On the one hand, there is our own will to believe that modern architecture is reformed and getting better, that the destruction of our cities has, if not halted, at least slowed, that the Great Mistake is over. On the other hand, there is our own sullen awareness that terrible things are still happening to our cities, terrible things that find their ocular proof, as Othello would say, in the growing ugliness of the cities themselves. So which will it be: our belief that something should be done about modern architecture or that nothing needs doing that modern architects aren't already doing for themselves?

The answer, oddly enough, depends on whether we rise to the challenge of the super-modern defence. We can run from it as too fearful and distracting. Or we can grab hold of it, partly as a geiger counter for discovering the true identity of the new modern architecture, partly as an Ariadne's thread that takes us out of the labyrinth of our modernist habits of mind to new alternatives that, seasoned and serviceable, can once again befriend a reawakened civic pride.

But I myself am slipping back into the once-new but now old way of thinking that got us into a modernist mess in the first place. I didn't mean of course to say new alternatives to modern architecture. I meant to say old alternatives that modernist habits of mind have crushed under foot. I too must unlearn and re-learn! But why not you as well? It's not too late! Didn't I always say it would take a book to correct your mistakes? Here is the book!

Yours ever, Conrad

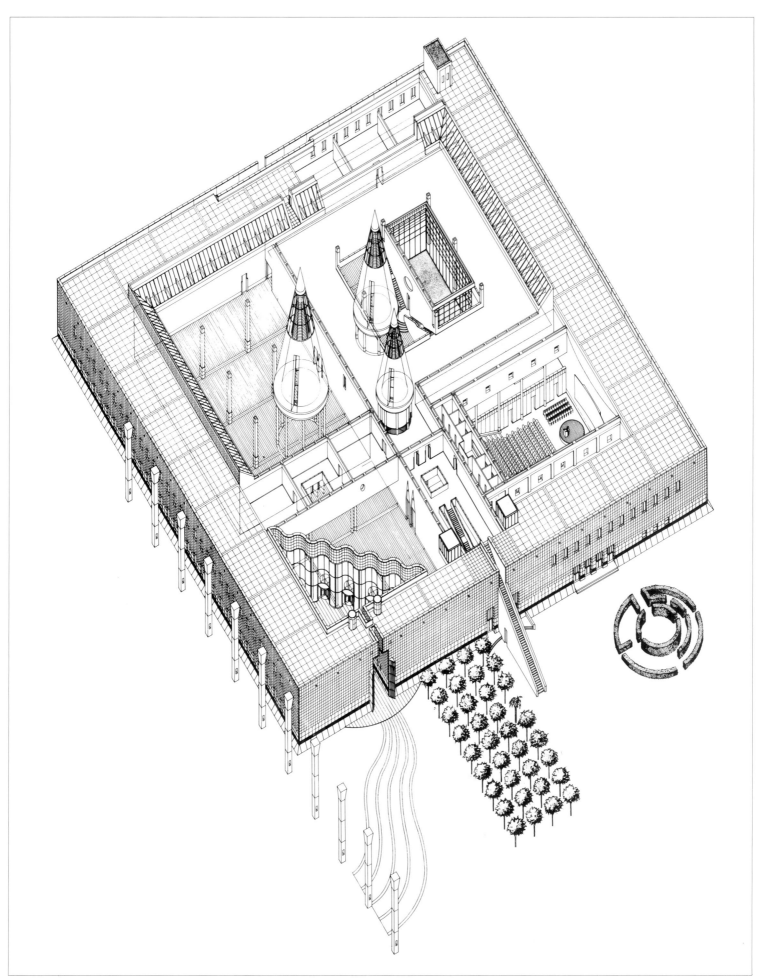

ART AND EXHIBITION HALL OF THE FEDERAL REPUBLIC OF GERMANY, BONN. AXONOMETRIC.

ROB KRIER

THE ARCHITECTURE OF GUSTAV PEICHL

Dear Gustav, you asked me to introduce your exhibition in London. Used to responding recklessly in your company I accepted the challenge. Of course my critical judgement is affected by the technical 'bias' I feel. True, problems between us are few when it comes to technical points of the building trade. But our philosophical and ideological positions are rather less than closely related. And the age gap of ten years between us enhances the difference in our generation-bound visions. You learned your trade in the 50s, I did in the 60s. And what's more, we come from different parts of Europe. What Central European may dare a thorough scrutiny of a Viennese soul? But you are a marked realist, so it is easier for me to access you than many another colleague here in Vienna. I just hope to find the proper definitions for our two art worlds, and I will not fail to hammer out and pronounce my judgement on the things we agree and disagree on.

Let's assume I would have to explain 'The Peichl Case' to my students – I would have to put him against my ideas and works, and this is the approach that I am going to take here as well. 'Peichl seen through the Krier glasses' or 'Peichl as Krier would like to see him'. 'What can I learn from Peichl?' or 'What is there for me to teach Peichl?'

Gustav, forgive me for the professorial note! But I do not address the honoured established colleagues who drink to your health at the opening of your exhibition and who compliment you with a false or real smile. They know you and they have long since milked your contribution in their publications and works. Instead it is the young ones who look at you and probe your oeuvre for its exploitability, if not copying value.

The art of 'imitation' has been one of the cardinal virtues of the traditional building trade. Things which could not be imitated or repeated lost their value and usefulness. This applied to classical details and continues to be a touchy issue as few basic physical construction principles have actually changed. Many architectural experiments of this century failed because new and untested techniques were used wrongly. Impudently they believed and at places still believe they could do without the experience of traditional architecture.

One compliment I can pay you without any reservation is on the quality of workmanship in function construction and detail exhibited by your buildings. This remark with its faint suggestion of criteria appreciated in Switzerland is an insult a *quantité négligeable* in Vienna. But here you are faced with a British audience used to heated discussions of architectural eyesores.The remark after all means not just that your roofs are waterproof, that no fungi attack the interior walls, that facade facings and windows do not drop out of their mountings making users risk their lives and limbs. Your buildings work properly because you have always searched for a clear and typical solution to your ground plans. The search for such quality necessarily leads to elementary geometrical forms whose spinal column holds easily locatable access and distribution systems.

You have never been afraid of applying the advantages of symmetric composition whenever they served the logical structure of the design. Inside you frequently stuck to those principles while externally you were usually tempted to suspend the severity. Like other colleagues from the 60s – Archigram or the Metabolists – you were a pioneer of the architectural theory of flexibility and growth potential. These ideas were valuable in filling the theoretical vacuum of the period. But reality soon put the plain fact of the building substance's immobility into its proper light again. Many promising talents foundered at these and other pale visions of society and architecture.

Peichl has never been a dreamer. He has been level-headed and speculative in utilising the themes. It is no coincidence that they produce a credible and marketable image for his ORF radio and TV studios. It seems that a media power and opinion-making instrument must not show its real face by putting up monumental representative buildings. Instead it prefers to duck in the landscape. A loose building mass appears as the perfect magic hood to hide the moloch. The towering antenna sculptures look rather like toy trinkets. I would have disguised the bear with the mask it deserved and would have promptly failed – then as now.

You hit the nail on the head with your scheme. The studios are indubitably among the most elegant prototypes of 1960s research. What bothers me slightly is the smooth perfection and rigidity of the Meccano system of thinking. If only you had had less money at your disposal. A touch of gruff artisanship would have done you good such as you showed at your phosphate elimination plant in Berlin. We really agree on this one! Peichl pulling himself together dismissing the glitter after the ORF series and simplifying his repertoire. Hardly any mention of adaptation, the buildings are tightened; his ORF studio extensions in Vienna and his museums in Frankfurt and Bonn breathe gravity and quiet.

Gustav this is the right direction. Here you will approach the poetry you have so often yearned for much more than with your technoid schemes. Enough of this to show my affection. I promised a lot of analytical stuff at the beginning. But I cannot keep my promise. It is asking too much. The exhaustive Peichl workshop should perhaps be continued by somebody who is more neutral. But oh my dear Gustav how much would I like to give you private lessons in urban town planning!

Let me just clarify my position *vis-à-vis* you. After the glamorous period of high-tech pranks which touched me marginally, if at all, I am much impressed by the Vaduz art house project, the Afienz radio satellite station, the ORF archives in Vienna (the best inside and out), the phosphate elimination plant in Berlin and the museums I already talked about.

You have ensured your technical survival. You have long since conquered the hearts of the modern English. I even believe you capable of convincing them that you as an Austrian and Holzmeister pupil know a lot about traditional building art – really and truly.   *Rob Krier, Vienna, November 1989.*

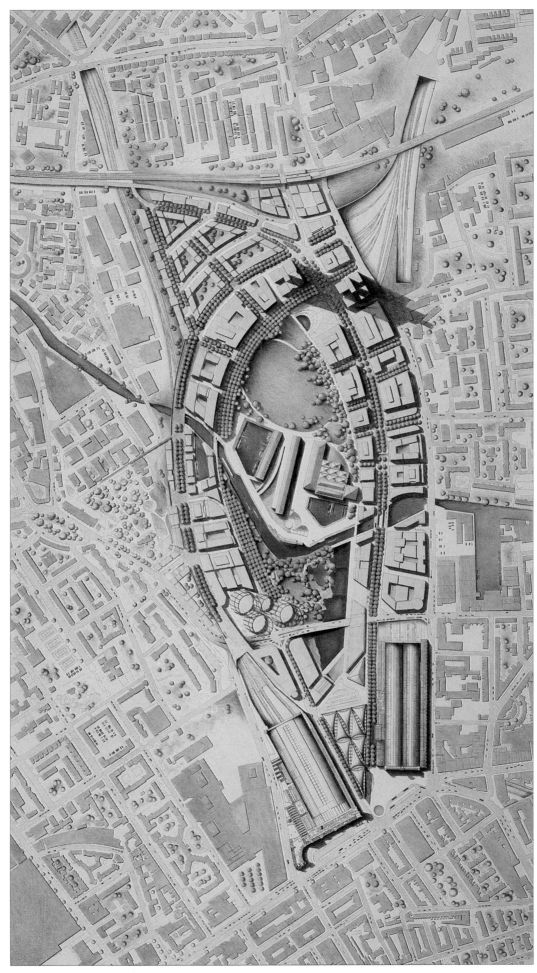

OVERALL PLAN OF THE MASTERPLAN AND THE SURROUNDING AREA

NORMAN FOSTER

KING'S CROSS
A Master Plan

MODEL, DETAIL OF TOWERS

Norman Foster introduces his proposals for Europe's largest development on this sensitive central London site. The full master plan incorporates his designs for a new roof canopy and twin spires in a scheme which involves both the work of other distinguished architects, and the renovation and rehabilitation of some existing structures, to create a richer mix of activities within the city centre.

This is a master plan, it is not a collection of definitive building designs – far from it, it is outline planning and a master plan. It seems to me that the group behind this exhortation to release more land for homes was perhaps a kind of plea to invade the countryside, the green belt and the kind of easy pickings of greenfield sites, and at the same time to avoid the desperate social and technical challenge of the inner city. If you look at decayed structures and indeed open land, there seems to be more than enough land to respond to the challenges of housing and other related activities, and King's Cross is very much in that inner city tradition. I know that it's rather fashionable to talk nostalgically about the drama and arrival above ground by rail into the heart of the metropolis, but I think it's a slightly mistaken view of the past because at the time of the invasion by railroads into the heart of cities, they were as brutalising in their own way as motorways and flyovers are today. I suspect that in the future people will look back and conclude that there's not too much Zen under a flyover any more than there is in the impact of the railways. I personally feel no great sense of loss having been brought up alongside the railway tracks, or of the prospect of an arrival essentially being below ground, and freeing up the area at ground level for people.

The King's Cross site is not as desperately desolate, closed and washed over by successive waves of change but certainly right for redevelopment and displays all the symptoms of the changes that have overtaken transportation, the many different ways of technological change and the very landlocked, huge site. It always surprises me that because it is a black hole, you can drive around and never really be aware of it. One of the challenges of the site was to permeate it, to establish its links and in the process of starting that examination, to be a little more precise around what the generators might be for a master plan. The generators would be the heritage buildings, the canal, the transportation infrastructure which in many ways generates the opportunity and the brief reminder of those generators, the classic frontal hotel, King's Cross, the King's Cross facade, St Pancras Hotel, the Great Northern alongside King's Cross, and the amazing train sheds that back on to them as well as the combination of the Regent's Canal and some very distinguished individual buildings, clusters of buildings, the granary by Cubitt, the coal drops, all around 1850. It was an amazing opportunity to preserve those, to re-create settings for them as vital ingredients in a master plan. London is really quite different in its grain from those gridded cities which might be American, like Chicago and New York, or European, like Barcelona and Paris. London is by the nature of its names – even a scan of the A-Z will produce, in any kind of random order: Islington Green, Shepherd's Bush, Regent's Park, St James' Park, Hampstead Heath. The list is

MODEL, DETAIL OF THE TERMINAL

endless; they all have connotations of green space, sometimes quite small, village-like in scale, other times large open tracts of land, with individual places relating to those highly personalised spaces, all loosely connected. That seemed to us an important clue around what might generate quite powerfully the master plan; an opportunity to create around it a green space, seen as a rather classical imposed oval. The long dimension of that park which extends from the southernmost part, almost physically touches the terminal to the south and extends to the northern boundary. The generators are the railway lines, the new low-level station which penetrates below the site and which would provide the facilities for the cross Channel link, the European terminus, the existing Midland mainlines, the east-coast mainlines, the new suburban lines on the left-hand side, the maze of London underground linkages which happen below the terminal.

The new terminal is a kite-shaped, triangular building and the landscaping comes right down either side of it. The park runs down to it. Below the terminus is a veritable, quite extraordinary three-dimensional maze which looks like an attempt at some deconstructivist building, but is an amazing spaghetti of fleet sewers, release sewers for the fleet sewers, the Metropolitan line, the pipes which are kind of ventilators. The challenge was really to lock into and be informed by this extraordinary three-dimensional below-ground maze and to produce something above ground that would have an urban simplicity relating harmoniously and complementing the two stations; to integrate and make one major rationalised terminus out of what was historically really a competitive two-station game of one turning its back on the other, the other trying to upstage and really being, in that sense, divisive both operationally and architecturally.

It is impossible for us not to be influenced by the work that we are currently doing at Bilbao on the new metro system there, where the eruption at the street level with the crystalling canopies is informed by the flow of escalators down to the stations. We are making a conscious effort to enlarge the below-ground stations into more generous halls with devices such as putting the ticketing in the main hall, suspending those and trying to re-examine the whole nature of an underground system. The needs in total, both operationally and symbolically, to make one station with its own clear, direct, minimum distance routing to the various levels below and connections across to platforms in St Pancras and King's Cross, needed one unifying element which had a clear statement of entrance and was capable of rationalising into one complex this one station idea. It was an opportunity, certainly in terms of King's Cross, to replace the bomb damage, bringing it back to its original splendour, not only on its flanks but also in much more dramatic terms. The idea was to have the terminus uncluttered by all the traditional dross of suspended ceilings, festooned tubes, moving air, dangling fluorescent lights, all the paraphernalia of that serviced roof and to pull those discreetly below ground, where in many ways they are better for access and servicing. We wanted to free that roof umbrella so that it could be much more to do with directing the water, the run off, whilst admitting the magic component of natural light; the streaks of sunlight into the heart of the space, the calm space with views, relationships with the sky, which one can see coming through in the early studies on the terminal at King's Cross. The photo-montage shows how that would provide a generously covered canopy with the area below it scooped out as a kind of amphitheatre where the steps would run, as the dimension got wider, on the curve into a natural ramp. Thus there wouldn't be a demarcation between steps and ramps making the disabled second class citizens but the thing would appear effortlessly integrated into one total entrance.

I could communicate the strategy of this master plan by examining it one part at a time and then like Humpty-Dumpty finally putting the whole thing together. On the route through from Pancras Road through to the existing gasholders, there are three listed gasholders which are physically connected. Further across to the east there's another group of gasholders, which are not all listed and what I find interesting is this dialogue between the train sheds and the gasholders, which are incredibly powerful sculptures. They are very striking, powerful, beautiful things. There was the possibility of moving one of those listed gasholders which has to be maintained anyway so, instead, why not use and exploit it and get some drama and occasion out of it by grouping it with that cluster of three on the western edge in such a way that you would then have the drama of driving through it and seeing through the mist the tower of St Pancras. Interestingly, it was one of the early ideas on the project which we never actually got to work until the last few weeks – literally in the nick of time. A cluster of gasholders would be positioned strategically next to the bridge which provides the east-west link. This endeavour would bring together not only architects and the best talent but would also specifically break down the highly questionable barriers that seem to exist about bringing talented European architects from Italy, Spain, France, Germany. Therefore an image of the bridge next to the gasholders could be a highly sculptural event in that entrance sequence. The route that is tree-lined moving through north across to the east is quite different and, again, informed by quite different generators; by the work on permeability, on movement, on linkage with adjoining areas, called the Camden Magnet. One of the dimensional comparisons that you can make about the route is with Regent's Street which is 25 metres wide and 18 high. The particular route in question is slightly wider at 27 metres and slightly higher. It has trees in the middle and also what a lot of people like to call the 'people mover', but I prefer the tram. The tram is in the middle with cars either side in a very traditional arrangement. Either side of the street is again the very traditional device of creating the kind of edge portico. There aren't many examples in London but one of the most pleasurable is the one which is outside the Ritz in Piccadilly. It doesn't really matter whether the sun is shining, or raining as is the case in this country, but it provides that degree of protection and enclosure. I think it's also quite a unifying element in that it can control a lot of the individual clutter of advertising. It can provide a public facade and then, as you penetrate it, different layers relating to the announcement of the individual shops, restaurants, offices are placed behind you because it sweeps and is on a curve. It is also quite helpful to make the analogy with Regent's Street, which is shorter if you take the dimension from Piccadilly to Oxford Circus. This is something like 0.9 of a kilometre whereas this space is in the order of about 1.3 kilometres. So there are some vital differences and yet there are interesting commonalities. Moving down from ten storeys the scheme drops down on the edge of the park and there is no road on that edge. So it is quiet, a soft deliberately blurred edge which we would hope would encourage its own growth of pavement cafes – that world of the French outside cafe where you get the blurring of edges between something which is not quite private: you haven't penetrated the cafe, you haven't gone through the door, you're not into the private area. It is not public in the sense that if, in this instance, you're out on the pavement, but it's a kind of semi-public, more organic space. I think that the possibility of those activities developing organically and spontaneously on the edges has the potential to give a certain rightness and variety to it. If you put those two edges together you can start to look at the totality of that master plan generated from the terminus at the south and culminating in the vertical features of two office spires. I wouldn't call them towers in the traditional sense, possibly because the word is so loaded with its implication of the worst of

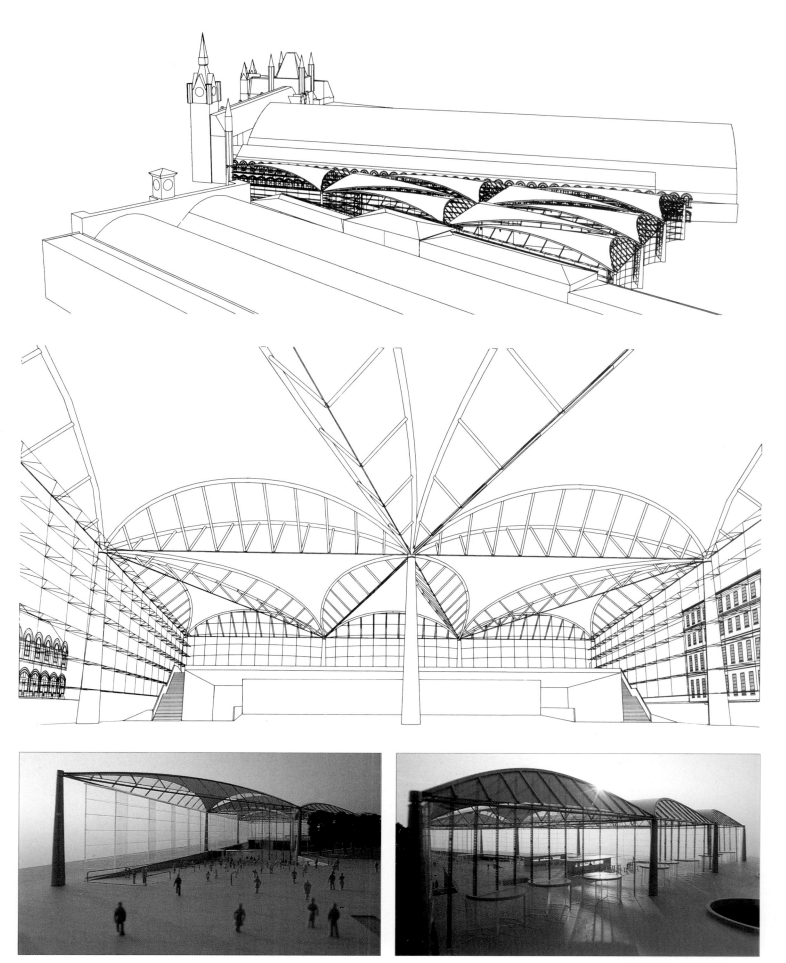

ABOVE: EXTERIOR PERSPECTIVE OF THE TERMINAL *CENTRE*: INTERIOR PERSPECTIVE IN THE TERMINAL *BELOW*: VIEWS OF TERMINAL MODEL

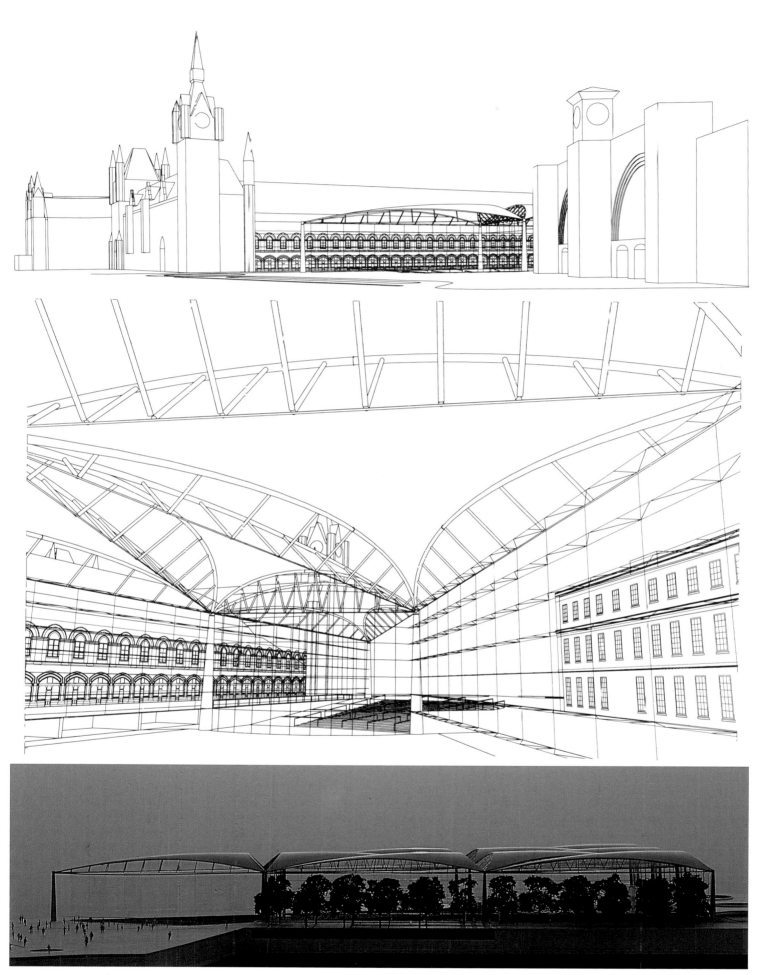

ABOVE: EXTERIOR PERSPECTIVE OF THE TERMINAL *CENTRE*: INTERIOR PERSPECTIVE IN THE TERMINAL *BELOW*: VIEW OF TERMINAL MODEL

the towers which have probably graced London more than most other cities and of anonymous slab blocks with no articulation, no breakdown of scale; monolithic, intimidating and anonymous. It had nothing to do with that at all but was instead a re-examination of what the office tower might be if you took it away from being the lowest common denominator of market values, if you actually had somebody as open-minded and courageous as the developers behind the scheme, to be open to totally new interpretations of what a cluster of office spires might be on the skyline, and limiting those to a group of two. It was once fashionable to justify some of those massive blocks which were not towers or spires at all; they had none of the aspect ratio, the slenderness that you would associate with the towers of San Giminiano. Quite rightly, the justification of using that image to draw an analogy has in many ways recently been rubbished. However, it doesn't deter me in the least from setting it as an example because I think it is quite interesting to see the way in which those individual elements, depending on how you move around, start to actually appear to physically join, and to see the breakdown of scale, the difference in height of these elements and the way they actually cluster on the skyline. I think it gives important clues around the possible nature of high-rise office buildings, because of the potential for interrupted transparency, the central core, which itself could be transparent with movement within it, and the office accommodation in segments which the lower platforms of, say, ten storeys, could occupy, at the base of the building, an appropriately large footprint and then, as you go higher, diminishing in five storey increments. It is quite a small sliver offering much tighter, more private accommodation in the upper reaches of the building while in the process creating platforms which could be gardens in the sky; they could be terraces, but give the potential for outside, open spaces. By picking away and, as it were, destroying that traditional kebab of repetitive spaces with the lift core embedded solidly in the heart of it, they offer some of the drama and liberation that one senses when moving up a structure like the Eiffel Tower where you are aware of both the city as it moves away from you and the skyline, so that a very dramatic relationship exists between you and the city. I was fascinated to see that one of the headlines was 'Two Eiffel Towers for London at King's Cross.' If the two towers have one eighth of the drama and sheer excitement of the Eiffel Tower then I think we will feel well rewarded by the headline. However, the form and shape is really somewhat different and we are still at the very early stages. There are diagrams to show some of the possibilities latent in the idea. Paley Park in New York, for example, is not suggested as being a transplant into the area but it evokes some of the possibilities of creating a high-quality public space related to that particular cluster and focus of accommodation. We have talked from day one about the desire to see a richer mix of activities so that this as a place would be active around the clock. It wouldn't be a particular major area that would go dead as the offices closed down, and then a particular area of housing which would be alive at some time and dead at others. The team have always felt it important to maintain the possibility of being able to exploit proximity and walking distances so that the two areas could in a way coexist cheek by jowl, and also to maintain the possibility of grouping a major portion of housing immediately adjacent to this area and starting to look at one kind of housing that could group around green courtyard spaces. In our work with some of the consultant architects and one firm in particular, Hunt Thompson, who have been doing a lot of study work on the housing at Maiden Lane, it comes with a lot of inherited problems and certainly there exists a very real potential to effect a degree of transformation by making this more accessible, physically linked to the new development so that it could have influence in all the right directions

rather than the idea of putting up barriers between one kind of development and another. A tremendous amount of research has gone into that whole question of linkage and permeability. If one moves across to the totally different subject of conservation and how some of those heritage buildings could be treated or transformed, then one of the major areas of celebration must surely be that the facade of King's Cross could for the first time actually be seen as fronting a major urban space, thus it could offer an opportunity for urban sculpture, for sensitive paving, contouring, relating to the movements of alighting points for buses and taxis. This would take away all those cobwebs which are not new and interesting. The incredible facade with its covered walk at the base is not actually the entrance and never has been – it has always been at the side. That prime facade has been civically vandalised in ages past, so it has probably been barely viewable for relatively few years. This is a pretty clear barometer of the need for extra space at ground level on this site. It is a very compelling indicator because basically if the architecture does not provide it in the first instance, then, one way or another, it is going to happen in reality. You may not like the way it will happen, but it will certainly be provided for.

An example of other views of conservation is the Germany gymnasium by Gruning. It was 1862 when this incredible interior was designed; that again will be released and realised by the stripping away of all mezzanines which have accrued in there, returning the gymnasium to its original splendour. It is important not only to be sensitive to the buildings but also, in a way, rediscover the settings for those buildings. An early drawing of the Granary building by Cubitt about 1950 shows the building related to a water basin which has since been filled in. Part of the master plan is to re-excavate those water basins creating a mixture of different kinds of water, the hard and the soft. With the recreation of hard water in the form of basins which are re-excavated, in some ways recreated and modified, the softer water as it goes south to the terminal, is much more about landscaping rather than hard brick edges. Housing is another ingredient which is added here, grouped around the water basin, as opposed to smaller wedges of housing which relate to the cross routes and to the offices. The water-based housing is generally distributed throughout the site to provide in the order of accommodation for some 5,000 people. The recreation, building up on what exists there of what I would call the hard water, the urban water, the canal systems and the basins associated with it, St James' Park demonstrates what I would call the soft water design, the ability of gaining a richer experience, that you can move as a pedestrian along the length of the park, starting with a walk that will take you through one kind of experience to another and finally through gardens, the Park and trees and so on, that is a network which is the structure of the site.

There is an amazing natural park, the Camley Park, which, despite all the extreme endeavours to avoid touching, is right in the path of the low-level station and the proposal there is, over time, to relocate to a more southerly location and then to create the opportunity for it to grow by a factor of 50%.

I have been comparing the movement across the park with that of Regent's Street. There will be a tram that will move the length of the site, together with a bus system which will service the side of the site. I think this is the gentlest intrusion compared with all the other devices that we looked at like monorails and underground systems which do have all kinds of level problems. The tram in so many ways seemed very gentle, human almost, one felt there was the potential for a sort of renaissance of the tram. I was very tempted to put a Blackpool tram for all kinds of personal, nostalgic reasons and also because I actually feel it is a very civilised tram, but in the end the version from Europe won.

If there are rediscoveries then the cycle is also very much a rediscovery of that whole sort of link; pedestrian and cycle routes that could permeate the site. I did talk about the ability of a waterway walk that can meander through the site, so that there would be quite a rich diversity of routes through large and small spaces. The master plan's coding indicates a richer mix of activities which are layered one on the other and adjoining each other. There is a reminder about the common denominator of the search for quality in the selection of the architects for the scheme. There is an opening-up of opportunities within this project in ways which everybody in Europe takes for granted, in that architects from adjoining European countries, including the United Kingdom, will be invited to contribute. So far this has not happened in one instance by any client whether public or private. King's Cross is an excellent opportunity and I am delighted to say that the developers are totally behind this. The aim is to bring together distinguished architects like Raphael Moneo who traditionally works in brick and Jean Nouvel. The list is a very long one, with specific architects whose skills would relate to the restoration, the re-creation, the regenerating of historic buildings like Jean Michel Willmot, for example, whose work in France in that field is quite extraordinary. There is also quite a long list of artists who would be involved in the project, including Sara Oldenberg and Richard Long.

I think that it was interesting that the park was an early concept and a very powerful generator. I remember a lot of the cynics who said immediately the project was won that the park would shrink. However, the first thing that happened was that it got slightly bigger and now it is even larger. We were never happy with the imposed oval which was very abstract; it related to a number of the generators but it was awkward. After a total re-examination we decided on a way in which the park could respond to the contouring, the bowl effect at the northern edge which would create a level change of some three metres, and the manner in which the sweep of a crescent follows the movement of trains below with the foundation implications of building on top and the station and lines which would run around it. The park would be somewhere where you could take the kids on Sundays, somewhere it would not be dead, but there would be a genuine interaction of a place where people could live and visit. It would be something with a local flavour, it would also have something that would relate to the movement of people on a large scale and would be international. I think, for all of us, this is very much a shared inspiration. As somebody said, cut it short and just say that you have to catch a train because one of your most important clients is British Rail. So, on that note I'll finish.

MODEL VIEW

———— * ————

43

Mick Jagger performing 'Miss You' at the autocue position, downstage centre. View from the spot platform on the stage-left lighting elevator

ROLLING STONES

After eight years the Rolling Stones are touring again. This time they have chosen the hard image of high tech architecture to complement their performance. At first sight the architectural set creates an impression of contemporary industrial decay which, during the show, is transformed into a theatrical experience of light and colour. Here we present commentaries from three personal view points.

Stage set under camouflage projection in the LA Coliseum during 'Harlem Shuffle'

MARK FISHER AND JONATHAN PARK

IT'S ONLY ROCK'N'ROLL

THE STEEL WHEELS NORTH AMERICAN TOUR

Mark Fisher

The opening concert of the Rolling Stones' eighth US tour in September 1989 marked a high point in the development of the art of outdoor rock performance. The stage set was the largest ever built for a rock concert. It was erected in 33 cities in 15 weeks.

The project required a travelling crew of 200 people, 86 trucks of equipment and local crews of 150 stagehands in each city. Mounting such a tour would have been impossible without the resources and expertise that have been built up in the rock

business since the Beatles played the first outdoor rock concert in Shea Stadium in 1965.

The concerts were seen by more than three million people in the USA, generating revenues exceeding $100m. The ability of bands like the

The concert is popular opera on a huge scale

Rolling Stones to mount such ambitious tours comes from the commercial power of what was once the rock counterculture. The invention and manufacture of this equipment has happened in parallel with the emergence of rock music as a major cultural force during the last 20 years.

The managers of performers like the Beatles and Elvis Presley were quick to realise that they could command audiences equal in size to the audiences for sports like baseball, ice hockey and football. The 60s saw massive investment in covered arenas and outdoor stadia to add to and replace pre-war facilities. It was natural for the managers and concert promoters to experiment with presenting bands in these buildings. The rebellious nature of rock music and the excitement of the audiences meant that the genteel attributes of conventional concert or dance-hall venues were inappropriate. At the same time, the music was based on the use of electronically amplified instruments which allowed the bands to play in larger venues. Rock concerts were organised in sports arenas in the early 60s, and bands were soon playing to audiences of more than 8,000 on tours in the USA.

Whether any of the audiences actually heard much music at these concerts is open to doubt, for the technology of sound reinforcement was in its infancy. However, the presentation of large-scale concerts in venues which were not designed for that purpose was shown to be possible, and profitable. Sports buildings had no stage lighting systems, and if public address (PA) systems were installed they were unsuitable for music reproduction. Outdoor stadia had no stages at all. Either the bands or the concert promoters were forced to buy the equipment they needed to present the shows, and to carry it with them on tour.

Easily portable lighting and PA systems did not exist in the early 60s. The large buildings required powerful PA systems, and the novel application meant that there was no established industry making them. The first systems were assembled from industrial amplifiers and hi-fi components. Conventional theatrical lamps were heavy and tended to fall apart, so lightweight lamps were developed to replace them. As touring in sports buildings became com-

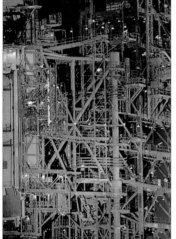

"Most of the audience only see the show once, so the stage set explores a range of intense emotions. It is like a building which is seen from dawn to sunset in two hours "

Above
The shuttle launch platform at the Kennedy Space Centre, an example of contemporary obsolete technology
Photo: courtesy NASA

Left
Preliminary sketch looking towards the stage-left PA tower, showing balconies and lighting gantries

Opposite, top
Preliminary sketch of the stage set showing the main form of a low roof between massive towers

Opposite, bottom
Preliminary sketch of the stage set showing proposed inflatables

monplace, a new service industry grew up to supply the necessary equipment. By the mid-70s, a network of hire and trucking companies had become established in the USA and Europe, mostly founded on the original investments by the first bands to tour, or by the promoters who organised the concerts.

Because bands were now playing in very large buildings, or in the open air, they were forced into a relationship with their audience which was quite different from the intimacy of a club or a theatre. In a theatre, the audience are relatively close to the stage, and the movements of the performers have a large effect on the scenic composition. In a stadium the audience have little choice of where they sit, and cannot move around to experience a different viewpoint. This is sufficient for sports, where the action spreads out across the playing area in dynamic patterns. But at a rock concert, the limited viewpoint and the great distances can make an orthodox stage performance very dull. As a result rock concerts became increasingly spectacular as the 70s progressed.

The stadia used for outdoor rock concerts are anonymous, remarkable only for their size. The most uncommon aspect of their interior spaces is the experience of sharing them with so many people, tiered up until the inner surfaces turn into mountainsides of human faces. When 60,000 people pay good money to assemble in conditions of discomfort and inconvenience their meeting is a demonstration of something which is important to them. The band is the focus of their shared identity, and the stadium becomes a temporary but tangible monument to these ideas, the background to a tribal rite. Rock stage design sets out to transform these inexpressive buildings into opera houses in which the performers establish an emotional relationship with their audience.

For their 1989 tour, the Rolling Stones wanted a stage which would reinforce their image as a tough, long-lived band still writing songs relevant to their audience. The early discussions about the design reflected contemporary preoccupations with the transition from the machine age to the information age. Stylistic references included the apocalyptic views of the future presented in films like 'Brazil', 'Blade Runner', and 'Black Rain', and in the novels of William Gibson. These pieces all share an extreme view of the built environment. The heroes inhabit cities in which the decaying slums of past cultures are overlaid with new monuments. Old buildings are too valuable, or too expensive, to demolish. Instead, they are 'retro-fitted' with the technology of the future, a romantic visual vocabulary in which high-tech overlays Victoriana, enjoying the visual delights of both. The novels of Gibson are more extreme than the visions in the films. The architecture is extended to include factories, Fuller domes and megastructures. These constructivist forms have lost any semblance of their original use; they are turned instead into bizarre forms of habitation and workspace. The power of the imagery lies in the contradictions of scale of that come from their reuse.

From the oil refineries of Yokohama to the shuttle launch platforms at the Kennedy Space Centre, the forms of obsolete industry are part of the Rolling Stones' audience's everyday lives. They are already monuments to dead technology; precursors of Gibson's world. The stage design places the band in a structure of ambiguous purpose created from these forms. It looks permanent, even though it is an alien and temporary ruin in the stadium. The industrial elements from which it is made are plainly non-functional. Their abandoned condition is a comment on the future, their portability an ironic aside.

The elements are realistic in modelling and scale, and unified by a patina of dereliction and decay which is visible by day, but lost under theatrical

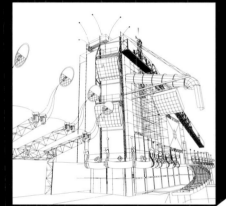

lighting. The baroque decorations on the balcony and the stage canopy are juxtaposed against them. They turn the composition into a fantasy, a monument to industry which does not belong in the present, the future or the past. Under theatrical lighting the monument evokes quite different moods, from post-holocaust cities to romantic bordellos. The decorations include a graphic identity which explored the imagery suggested by 'Steel Wheels', the title of the album which was released shortly before the tour. It was derived from a motif created from broken compact discs, circular saw blades and perforated metal, and was developed in parallel with the stage design.

The organization of the stage derives from the choreography of the band's performance and the technical requirements of the lighting and sound systems. The main performance area is an open plaza between two scaffolding towers. The 500kw PA forms two large masses which punch through the centres of the towers with the topmost speakers 20m above the ground. Panels decorated with Steel Wheels supergraphics hang inside the PA towers on different planes, and video screens for closed-circuit TV are built into the scaffolding at different heights. The bases of the towers are extended into balconies, terraces and stairs which allow the band to perform across the whole width of the stadium on different levels. The articulation of the balcony is reinforced by balustrading of swagged chain-mail and oversized balusters. The balusters are decorated with the Steel Wheels motif. The balcony makes a strong horizontal statement which finishes the base of the towers and allows the more articulated vertical forms to rise off a solid visual support. The Steel Wheels motif is also applied to the finials of the canopy which cantilevers over the performance area.

Above, top
Production sketch looking towards stage left with proposals for additional decoration

Above
Autocad drawing of the stage and PA tower from stage right. The 50kw lighting frames can be seen built into the elevator above the balcony and suspended from the snoot. The performance platform is visible on top of the PA tower

Opposite
View of the production model from stage right

Right
Mick Jagger testing the downstage monitors during soundcheck in the CNE Stadium, Toronto. Stage-right PA tower, balcony and snoot visible behind

Girders and ducts are hung off the scaffolding. These elements are functional, containing lights which illuminate the structure and the band, and symbolic, copying industrial forms. Because the stage set has no moving scenery, most changes of mood in the visual presentation are achieved by the lighting. The lights are placed to take advantage of the strongly articulated structure. The main mass is defined by bulkhead fittings of various colours which are placed on the girders and walkways. Eighty computer-controlled moving lights and 100 fixed lights, all with colour changers, are built into the girders, the handrails, and into the finials of the canopy. Eight 2.4m square frames, each containing 50kw of lights and fitted with colour changers, are mounted on the girders above the performance area. The movements of the musicians are tracked by ten follow-spots on stage and twelve in the stadium.

The itinerary for the Steel Wheels tour evolved in response to the availability of stadia in the cities where it was to play. Once the itinerary was fixed, the production coordinator organised the complex logistics which were necessary to get the crews and equipment to each venue and ensure that construction was completed by showtime. The work of the crews was so time sensitive that it became an extension of the performance by the band. Each concert really began with the arrival of the first truck of scaffolding, reached a climax as the band arrived, and ended when the last truck left. The construction program required four separate crews to build the scaffolding sub-structure eight or nine times during the 15 weeks. Each crew of 14 worked with about 70 crew hired locally in each city. The scaffolding was fitted out with one of two sets of scenery, PA and lights. This equipment arrived 36 hours before the concert, accompanied by its own supervising crew of 40 and 80 local stagehands. Twenty-four hours before the show the band gear, video equipment and instruments arrived, also accompanied by a separate crew of 40. The band, with their entourage of make-up, wardrobe and security, arrived on the afternoon of the show.

The concert opened with an explosion of flame projectors across the 100m wide frontage of the stage. The spectacle that followed was punctuated by a series of dramatic moments which reinforced the music. Some were created by the lighting, and others by special effects. 7kw slide projectors were used to camouflage the structure with Steel Wheels supergraphics during several songs. Instant inflatables accompanied 'Honky Tonk Women', and Jagger appeared on top of a PA tower for the opening of 'Sympathy for the Devil', with the whole structure bursting into flames beneath him. At the climax of the last song a coruscating pyrotechnic display started at the base of the structure and finished in the sky overhead.

The Steel Wheels tour delivered a major piece of music and theatre to over three million people in 15 weeks. The concerts were produced in outdoor stadia which had never been designed for the presentation of live music. They transformed these barren sports fields into fantastic landscapes using the most sophisticated technology available today, most of it purpose-built for the rock business. But the technology was only a background for the band. The paradox is that in the end the shows came down to the Rolling Stones, their music and their audience.

"The stage is a piece of guerilla architecture

Top
Detail of the stage-left balcony showing balustrading

Bottom
The stage on the afternoon of showday; CNE Stadium, Toronto

Opposite, top left
Stage-right snoot under construction during rehearsal at JFK Stadium, Philadelphia. The snoot is being lifted into place using chain hoists

Opposite, top right
View of the stage set from an auditorium follow-spot position; Shea Stadium, New York

Opposite, bottom
Stage-right girder under construction. The girders are assembled on the balcony and lifted up by chain hoists built into the PA tower. The crossheads from which the girder is suspended are visible at the top of the scaffolding

which transforms a football stadium into an instant temple for a night"

JAGGER

In Response to Questions
by Andreas Papadakis

"HIGH TECH IS NOT A BRAND NEW THING, IT IS A STYLE WE'VE SEEN FOR DECADES BUT IT STILL LOOKS CONTEMPORARY"

View of the stage from the
performance platform on the top of
the stage-left PA tower;
Pontiac Silverdome

This stage looks most strange when you're in the outdoor stadium. You go to the very back, to the top row, which is very high up, and you can see, above the stage, all the freeways, factories, and office blocks. It looks very peculiar within that urban structure and that's when it looks best.

When I first started talking about the set design, I was anxious to get away from the stage we had in 1981-2. That was rather a Memphis-style backdrop, with very bright colours and pictures of cars and guitars, which was very effective. We did a lot of outdoor daytime shows with it, but I wanted to get away from that and do something a bit different. My first thoughts were to have a three-dimensional, rather than just a painted backdrop, to fit in with the very large areas of football and baseball stadiums. I started thinking that on the one hand I wanted it to look like a city, but on the other hand I wanted it more like a forest. I had all kinds of mad ideas for this and eventually I went to three designers that I knew. (There're only really three or four people who work in Rock and Roll, who have done anything on this kind of scale. Although I like using people who aren't in Rock and Roll for the detail, I don't like using them for the major things because they just don't understand the visual nature of it and what's been happening before.) So I went to the three people and asked them to do sketches and ideas around the themes that I'd talked to them about. I knew Mark from his design for Pink Floyd *The Wall* which was an interesting piece and very similar to the kind of idea that I had. In the end, when I looked at the designs, I found that Mark's was the most fascinating. Then we started to work on it, with myself and Charlie Watts (who's the Drummer for the Rolling Stones), and we started to evolve the design. I gave Mark a starting point for my ideas, then he came back with his version of it, and we would go back and forwards, back and forwards, changing the colours and so on.

We have to remember that it's a performing stage, not just a piece of sculpture, so it has to actually physically work, from a practical point of view – for the performers, for the lights, for the audience, for the side lines, for moving it around – it has to come to pieces, it has to be trucked all over America. It is not just as if you were doing it for an exhibition, where you put the work up once and leave it up for three months and then take it down. This set has to be much more practical than that.

We worked very much as a team with Patrick Woodroffe, the lighting designer, and the sound man, because part of the set consists of light and sound equipment, and that all has to work together. We had the performers represented by myself and Charlie and the lighting and sound people all really working on it and throwing in ideas. It is very much a group effort, although Mark is the one who translated my original ideas into his vision of it.

So, as far as the relationship between music and stage design is concerned, it's just very much one thing. First of all you see the stage when you come in, it's not masked in any way, you walk right into the place and there you see it. Therefore the stage is a very strong statement which sets the tone of the show. The music and visual aspect are one thing. I don't actually think you separate them. You see the lighting and the stage, and hear the music all at the same time so when you come out you say 'Well that was a great show'. You don't say the light was good and the song was good or whatever, you've had a good time for whatever reasons. They are all very much the same thing, which is why collaborating very early on makes good sense.

I thought that 'Steel Wheels' was a good title for a moving show. In reality, as far as technology's concerned, it's very 19th-century. I was a bit

Wall of red flame projectors at the opening of the concert; Veterans Stadium, Philadelphia

aware of that, but I still think that it was a good title. The set is a glamorised version of the urban landscape – you can make of that what you will. Mark likes to talk of that at great length; I like to leave it to people to make their own connections. I could make a lot of pretentious nonsense about it but it obviously is a glamorised version, a lit version of something that you might see in an industrial city. The lighting is what makes it really interesting. It is a great statement when you see it on it's own, but when you see the design lit, it becomes more romantic. We took a lot of the lighting from images we had of the space shuttle taking off and being lit at night. We found those rather fascinating, so we thought, we could see how to light our set from those images.

The design for the set reflects the environment in which the songs were created. The themes for the songs are quite different, sometimes they're very romantic, sometimes they're very hard.

I quite like being in this environment for work. I find it a very stimulating environment to perform in, but I'm not sure whether I'd like to live or sleep in it, although I've noticed the crew sleep in it – they put hammocks up, underneath the various areas; they live in it more than I do! It's quite funny to see them all living in it, making tea, eating, sleeping and just living. I don't see the stage as being anarchic – I mean it's quite organised, it's a working environment. It is harsh though – it doesn't have any soft edges, there's no velvet, no nice sofas. That suits the music, which is what I wanted, something tough. I felt that the last tour was rather soft, but it worked for the show we were doing, which was a lot of sunny afternoon concerts, so it worked really well. This was evening/night stuff and I thought it was going to be harder. That's how it really started off.

I like traditional architecture very much but I like modern architecture too – I like modern environments. I don't particularly like trying to live in the 18th century all the time, although I do have an 18th-century house which is very nice to live in, but I don't mind living in a contemporary environment either;

I like to be able to experience both things. I do think that films, for instance, influence what people want to live in. When you see something on a film you might say 'I wouldn't like to live in that'. I don't know what an audience would think after coming to see to our show. Maybe they would imagine living with colours like this or lights like that; I don't really know what they think.

I don't know if we are trying to communicate a positive message about urban existence. We all live in the suburbs – Rock and Roll is very suburban. Most people who come and see the show probably live in the suburbs. No-one lives in the cities any more.

I like performing in the set. I don't think of it as an oil refinery (as it has been described), it's just very industrial and very hard. I am aware of that, but I still have to perform romantic songs and the lights transform it into a more romantic setting for those.

I think the thing about the design is that I love making these visual statements. It is nice to do music and so on, but I do get a lot out of making these very large visual statements. When you come in and see a large stage like this, then see the show on it, you probably think 'I remember that show'. You don't really remember details, you just remember how good the show was. I think the set, the lighting and design all contribute. People who come back next time will say 'I wonder what they're going to do *this* time'. It is very important to make those visual statements in such a large concert. I know one of Mark Fisher's points is that these 50, 60, 70,000 people are in another environment for one evening, and they're making a small town. It *is* an architectural statement and it's obviously got it's roots in technological architecture. High tech is not a brand new thing, it is something we've seen for decades but it still looks contemporary, so this style has kind of lasted.

It would be interesting to find out what the audience thinks of it. I've seen it for months –I've been living with it since March. I wonder what someone who comes in and sees it for two hours and then leaves thinks of it.

It's kind of interesting – I'm gonna ask some of them.

Left
Mick Jagger on top of the stage-left PA tower during 'Sympathy for the Devil'

Bottom
Aerial pyrotechnics during the finale; LA Coliseum

Below
The stage set bursting into flames during 'Sympathy for the Devil'; LA Coliseum

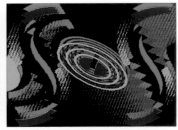

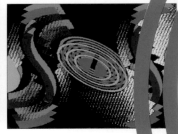

Close up of supergraphic projection on the stage-right PA and staircase

Close-up of the stage showing the roof and balcony under red light

Steel Wheels supergraphic camouflage during 'Little Red Rooster'. The image is projected by four cross-fading 6kw Pani projectors

Pyrotechnics exploding across the structure during the closing bars of 'Jumping Jack Flash'

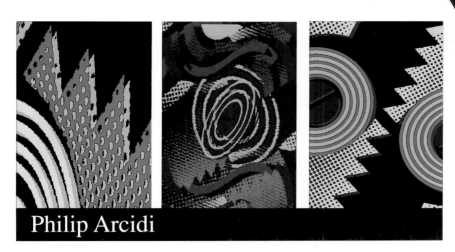

Philip Arcidi

TIMELY ADJUSTMENTS:

White look during 'Start Me Up'; LA Coliseum

We're used to hea... ...North America to hear the Rolling ...ven era has bur... ...Stones... May... ...Blues-inspired rock ...to the sidelines; t... ...to the benefit of the archi-...to give scant attention t... ...tectural profession, they're also wit-..., and prefers instead to t... ...ness to a heroically-scaled *scaena* popular culture, a more lively... ...that raises questions about our cul-...rometer of society's condition. Th... ...tural survival, with some compelling it should hearten architects to see theatrical effects. that the Steel Wheels tour, one of the

As they approach their concert seats, decade's most successful rock con- spectators confront a 300-foot wide cert tours, brings an estimated three platform surmounted by rambling million people face to face with an steel frames and light towers eight impressive stage designed by the storeys high. Once the performance Architect Mark Fisher. Spectators begins, the set comes to life; it flashes are filling football stadiums across banks of lights in an endless array of

patterns, bellows smoke, transmits videos of the musicians, inflates a pair of balloon giantesses, and fi- nally erupts in a pyrotechnic shower. Like the music, it's great entertain- ment.

A scaffold that resembles an abandoned factory with high-tech implants, the stage set won't be eas- ily forgotten by the audience. To this concert goer, it recalled the 1960s and 70s, and the realisation that a generation has passed since the baby boomers' counter-culture challenged the conventions of their parents.

Video excerpts of performances long past, the lined faces of the musicians, and the set's faux-ruin imagery at- tested to our advanced years.

The ironies of presenting a rock and roll band on a stage that heralds the obsolescence of modern industry are probably obvious to architects. They're likely to consider the set a descendant of the work of Archigram, the collaborative of British archi- tects who celebrated technology as a social liberator. Unlike his predeces- sors, however, Fisher (and the Roll- ing Stones, who collaborated) offers

RETROFIT TECHNOLOGY

Top
Purple look in 'Rock and a Hard Place', with special film running on the video screens; LA Coliseum

Middle
Blue look from stage left; RFK Stadium

Bottom
Mick Jagger on the stage-right balcony

no premonitions of an immanent utopia. Towering steel frames, which Peter Cook, Ron Herron, Christine Hawley, and others in the Archigram studio designed as gleaming icons of a new urban order, are here rendered as desolate hulks, appended by a fractured satellite dish and a pair of dangling metal smokestacks.

Although we rarely find any more proposals for cities that walk, fly, or float, Fisher is regaling massive audiences with a computerised display of electronics and video images that Archigram envisioned, but never realised. The Steel Wheels set is programmed with a different lighting pattern for each song; as the music changes, so does our perception of the stage's space and structure. Its profile is outlined by blinking pinpoints of light; banks of floodlights, wrapped by conveyor belts of gels, sometimes define the structural frame

which seems to lose its three-dimensionality and become a silhouette. Foreground and background, as well as solid and void, are continually reconfigured with new arrays of illumination. Fisher's incandescent illusions prove Archigram's proposition that a space need not be defined by solid enclosures: he brings to North American football stadiums a fragment of Idea City: immaterial entities - music, lights, and projected images - have become a medium for marking a place

Stadiums filled with 50 or 60,000 ticket holders are the norm for the Steel Wheels tour. While impressive to business managers, these figures could be disastrous for the performance; it is difficult to sustain the musicians' presence across a 30,000 square-foot playing field. At their suggestion, Fisher extended the concert stage so that it straddles the

Above
Psychedelic multicolour look in '2000 Light Years'; CNE Stadium, Toronto. The look is achieved by using liquid colour wheels in 6kw Pani projectors

Bottom Right
Close-up of the stage during rehearsal in the rain; JFK Stadium, Philadelphia

Also on these pages; Projection supergraphics of the "Steel Whhels" motif

grandstands and extends into the audience. The breadth of the stage and the irregular composition of its backdrop imply that the performers' space is tailored to blend into its surroundings; in reality, it does not. For all its bulk and elaboration, the Steel Wheels set is a fixture geared for rapid assembly and dismantling; its self-contained design was mandated be prerequisites of flexibility.

Two huge video screens (supplemented by a third located in the playing field) bring images, if not the musicians themselves, into viewing range for the audience. Like a wall of videos in a nightclub, the screens multiply the performers' presence with a succession of rapid-fire images generated by mobile cameras. Close-up shots, interspersed with clips from previous performances and video productions, provide pleasant distractions; spectators are free to

shift their focus from the performers to the stage set or screen images. Though ostensibly satisfying, this visual barrage does not fully mitigate the distended nature of the stadium-scaled performance. Cinematic shots of the Rolling Stones offer a photographic duplicate, rather than the musicians themselves; facsimilies are not a substitute for the exchange that resonates between performers and their audience.

Twenty years ago, the Stones would have commissioned this stage without any thoughts of the unrelenting mark of time; like their young contemporaries, they perhaps believed that they had sidestepped the continuum of history. In those years, the legacy of their predecessors seemed irrelevant, as did their inevitable replacement by a succeeding generation. By the simple act of survival, the Stones have had to ac-

knowledge that time has changed them, as it does everything else. Now they face the task of regenerating the creative fusion that has yielded some of the most memorable musician in rock and roll.

Fisher's concert stage is emblematic of the way the Rolling Stones, and perhaps their generation, sees itself today: a building which once embodied a revolutionary culture has become worn with age. Stripped to its structure, it finds itself host to an array of novel technology, old and new are combined, generating a force-field of lights, sound and moving pictures. A metamorphosis has taken place. Through an art of self-renewal, the building has extended the life-span, and forestalled time's desolation.

Above Right
'2000 Light years'
seen from the press
gallery level; LA Coliseum
Far Right
Keith Richards and
Ron Wood

Above
Backstage view
showing Charlie Watts
during sound check;
Sullivan Stadium, Foxborough

Left
Two views of the stage with
alternate colours on the
balcony balustrade. The
colour changes are made
with Vari*Lites mounted on
the balcony handrail

Right
Stage-right Honky Tonk
woman being tested during
sound check in Shea
Stadium. The inflatable
women are 16m high and
inflate in 30 seconds

Far Right
Stage-left Honky Tonk
woman, with Mick Jagger
and the Uptown Horns

Production designed by *Mark Fisher, Jonathan Park, Patrick Woodroffe, Mick Jagger, Charlie Watts, and Michael Ahern*

Set design: *Fisher Park Limited*
Lighting design: *Patrick Woodroffe*
Production Coodination: *Michael Ahern*
Sound engineer: *Benji Lefevre*
Monitor engineer: *Christopher Wade-Evans*
Steel Wheels motif and stage
graphics: *Mark Norton*

Graphic design by Mark Norton, 4i Collaboration
Photographs and sketches by Mark Fisher

DANIEL LIBESKIND
THE JEWISH EXTENSION TO THE GERMAN MUSEUM IN BERLIN

MPLEX FROM LINDENSTRASSE

BETWEEN THE LINES

A Museum for the City of Berlin must be a place where all citizens, those of the past, of the present and of the future, must find their common heritage and individual hope. To this end the Museum form itself must be rethought in order to transcend the passive involvement of the viewer: actively confronting change.

The extension of the Berlin Museum with a special emphasis of housing the Jewish Museum Department is an attempt to give voice to a common fate: common both to what *is* and what is *not*. The Museum must not only serve to inspire poetry, music and drama, (etc.) but must be the threshold of the ordered-not-disordered, chosen-not-chosen, silent-not-silent.

The particular urban condition becomes the spiritual site wherein the nexus of Berlin's precarious destiny is at once mirrored, fractured and transformed.

The past fatality of the German-Jewish cultural relation in Berlin is enacted now in the realm of the not visible. It is this invisibility which must be brought to light in order to give rise to a new hope and to a shared inner vision. Thus this project seeks to reconnect Berlin to its own history which must never be forgotten.

Great figures in the drama of Berlin who have acted as bearers of a great hope and anguish are traced into the lineaments of this museum: Heinrich Kleist, Rahel Varnhagen, Walter Benjamin, E.T.A. Hoffman, Friedrich Schleiermacher, Arnold Schoenberg, Paul Celan. They spiritually affirm the permanent human tension which is polarized between the impossibility of System and the impossibility of giving-up the search for a high order. Tragic premonition (Kleist), sublimated assimilation (Varnhagen), inadequate ideology (Benjamin), mad science (Hoffman), displaced understanding (Schleiermacher), inaudible music (Schoenberg), last words (Celan); these constitute the critical dimensions which this work as discourse seeks to transgress.

The new extension is conceived as an emblem. The invisible has made itself apparent as the Void, as the not visible. Void/Invisible: these structural features have been gathered in this space of the City and laid bare. An Architecture where the unnamed remains: the names keep still.

The existing building is tied to the extension underground, preserving the contradictory autonomy of both on the surface, while binding the two together in depth. Under-Over-Ground Museum. Like Berlin and its Jews, the common burden – insupportable, immeasurable, unshareable – is outlined in the exchanges between two architectures and forms which are not reciprocal: cannot be exchanged for each other.

The urban, architectural and functional paradox of closed/open, stable/added, classical/modern, museum/a muse, is no longer reconcilable through some theoretical utopia and can no longer presuppose the fictitious stability of State, Power and Organization. In contrast, the paradox presupposes the not-visible, i.e. transformation, directly out of that which would exclude the visible appearance and the not-visible disappearance alike.

What all this amounts to is two lines: one straight but broken into pieces . . . the other tortuous but continuing into infinity. As the lines develop themselves through this limited-infinite 'dialectic', they also fall apart – become disengaged – and show themselves as separated so that the absence centrally running through what is continuous, materializes itself outside as ruined, or rather as the solid residue of independent structure, i.e. as a voided-void.

The distant and the gaping mark the coherence of the work because it has come apart: in order to become accessible (both functionally and intellectually). What was from both inside and out never pre-existed as a whole (neither in the ideal Berlin or in the real one) nor can it be put together again in some hypothetical future. The spacing is the sundering, the separation brought about by the history of Berlin which can only be experienced as the absence of time and as the time fulfillment of space no longer there.

The ultimate event of history – the Holocaust – with its concentration space and annihilation – the burn-out of meaningful development of Berlin and of humanity – shatters each place while bestowing that which no one can give: reserves of sacrifice, the offering: vigilant night-watch over absent and future meaning.

Urban Design Concept
The proposal gives new value to the existing historical context by transforming the urban field into an open, future-oriented urban matrix. The proposed extension is characterized by a series of real and implied transformations which go beyond the existing forms of the site. The compactness of the traditional street pattern is gradually dissolved from its Baroque origins and related diagonally to both the housing developments of the sixties and the new I.B.A. projects.

The new structure reasserts the urban importance of the 'Collegienhaus' and through a series of contrasts engages the existing housing and public structures in a new dialogue. Thus the proposal creates an intense field whose old boundaries withdraw, exposing the vitality and multi-dimensionality of Berlin.

Organization of the Building and the Required Functions
The new extension provides the Berlin Museum with an entire set of new and flexible spaces. These spaces act in series of 'open narratives', which in their architecture seek to provide the museum-goer with new insights into the collection, and in particular, the relation and significance of the Jewish Department to the Museum as a whole.

The Jewish Department is closely interwoven with the rest of the collection, yet is entirely independent and can be experienced alone as an integrated whole: both outside and inside, and both from the outside and from the inside.

Standard exhibition rooms and traditional public spaces have been dissolved and disseminated along a myriad of complex trajectories in, on, and above the ground. These trajectories gradually and systematically transform themselves in their form, function and significance.

Linear structures interact to create an irregular and decisively accentuated set of displacements, providing an active path and distancing the viewer in the investigation of the exhibits. These may be arranged both horizontally (plan), vertically (section), or in combinations of the two.

Walls contain functional and circulation elements (stairs, services, and funicular platforms) as well as 'walled-in' meditation spaces for the presentation of audio-visual materials.

Library books are disposed along the walls to become part of the exhibits themselves, wherever necessary.

The lecture room is transformed into a dynamic 'mechanical theatre' by the movement of a single platform. This offers the possibility of truly spatial-kinetic exhibits, and puts the audience into a new relation to performance.

The restaurant is set in relation to the underground Museum connection. It is independently accessible and works in juxtaposition to the Bierstude in the 'Collegienhaus'.

The Museum ensemble is thus always on the verge of *Becoming* – no longer suggestive of a final solution.

Link to the Existing Building
The link between 'Collegienhaus' and the new extension is made through the central spine of the old building re-establishing this stair in its original Baroque position. The underground Jewish Berlin collection thus serves as the 'interchange station' between the different levels of the Museum and the collection itself. In this way, the 'Collegienhaus' is restored and preserved in its autonomy, while becoming all the more integrated with the new building.

Fragments of the Museum – in the form of indeterminate closed/open voids – lodge themselves in all parts of the territory to become dispersed traces suggestive of past and future public use.

In this way, the link itself becomes – as connection – the structural key to the full integration of the underground galleries, restaurant, external Museum fragments, the extension, and the disrupted interior.

Structure. Materials, and Facade Design
Structure: Pre-cast and cast-in-place concrete elements, constituting a tube with variable inclination.
Cladding: Various cladding materials including metal, mosaics, and glass. Special emphasis (see elevations) on light quality and lumination control.
Facade Design: Richly textured, visually de-naturalized, luminous surface, creating tension between the hand and the eye.

Concept for Open Spaces, Parking
E.T.A. Hoffman plaza whose focus in the 'Mechanical Garden of Olympia' this moving image of Berlin is projected on four planes, 49 cubes, 196 surfaces and 98 hidden facets. The spectacle is

MODEL. VIEW FROM ABOVE

oriented for the benefit of the museum-goer, but is also accessible to the public at-large outside of the Museum and in the Restaurant.

To be included in the rotation: 1. Atrani: The gently rising baroque staircase leading to the church; 2. Navy: Children's playground in the form of tall sailing ships; 3. Versailles Facade: Closely cropped planting and topiary; 4. Heidelberg Castle: Ruins jutting into the sky; 5. Seville, Alcazar: Wooden dance platform; 6. Marsailles Cathedral: A sleeping car to eternity; 7. Freiburg Munster; 8. Moscow, Saint Basil's: Life-size wooden dolls; 9. Boscotrecase: Stone-pine forest; 10. Naples, Museum Nazionale: A child holds out freshly picked flowers; 11. Florence Baptistry: Helplessly stretched arm reaching for a fruit that remains beyond the reach; 12. Sky: A line, a Maiden, a Scale; 13: Polar Sea.

The 'fresh-air corridor' includes the children's playground, pedestrian paths and the anticipated bicycle pathway. Above-ground parking on a reinforced grass filed for 53 automobiles.

MODEL, VIEW FROM ABOVE

67

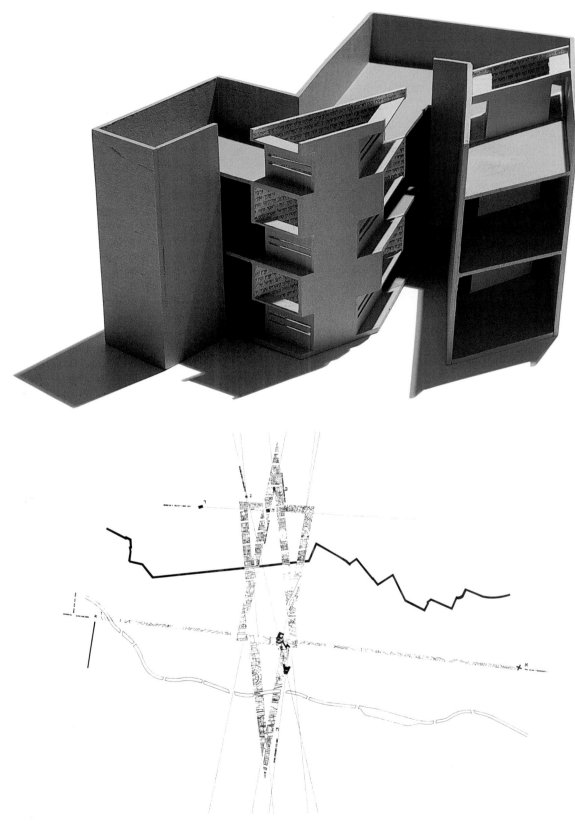

ABOVE: MODEL, INNER STRUCTURE OF THE BUILDING; *BELOW*: PLAN OF THE URBAN SCALE WITH THE INVISIBLE AXIS

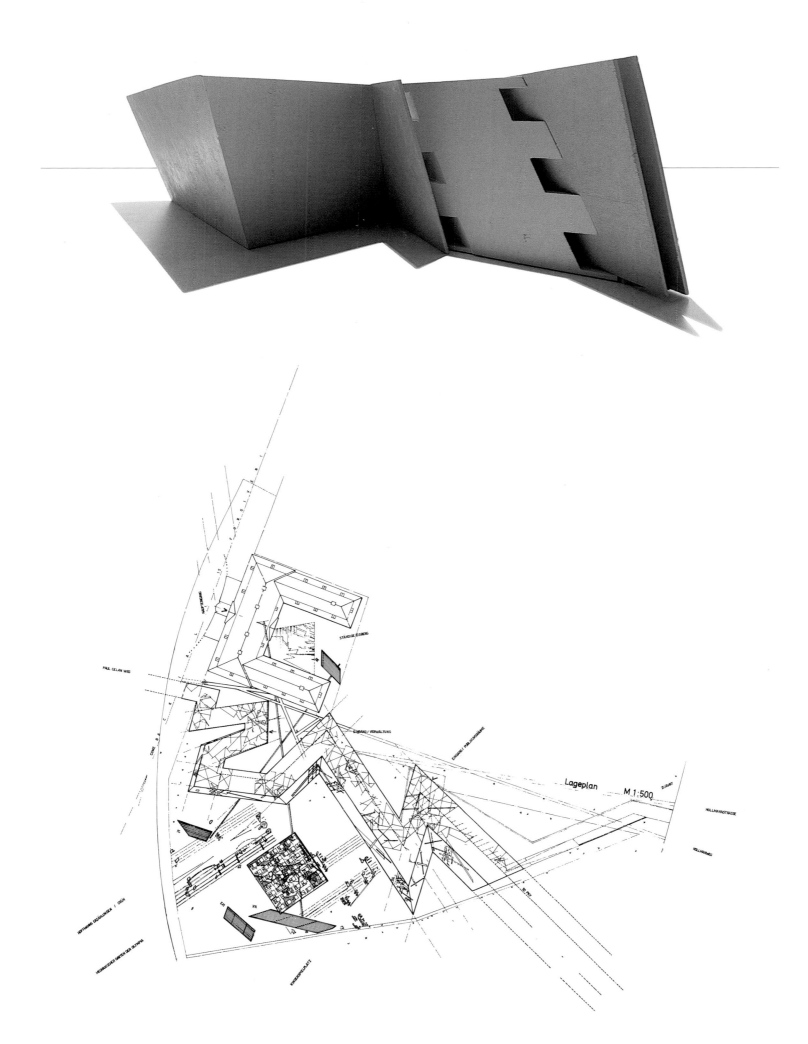

ABOVE: MODEL, INNER STRUCTURE OF THE BUILDING; BELOW: SITE PLAN

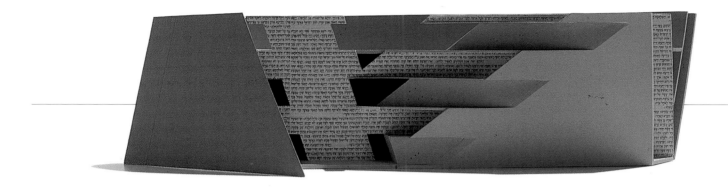

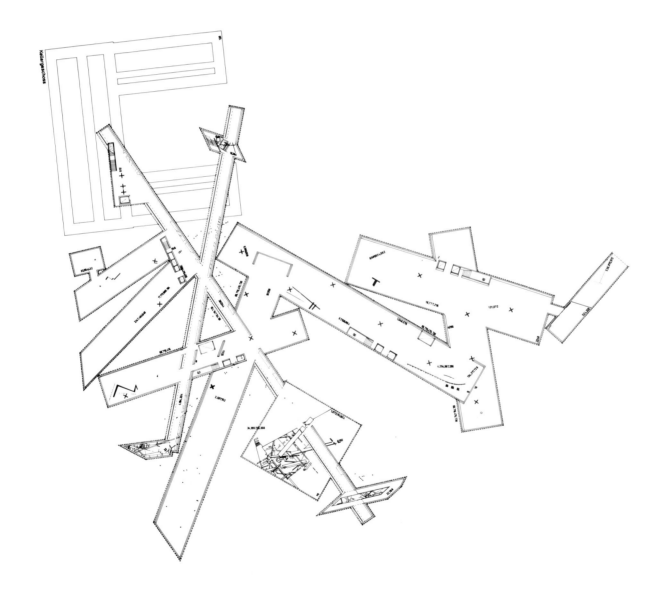

ABOVE: MODEL, INNER STRUCTURE OF BUILDING; *BELOW*: BASEMENT PLAN

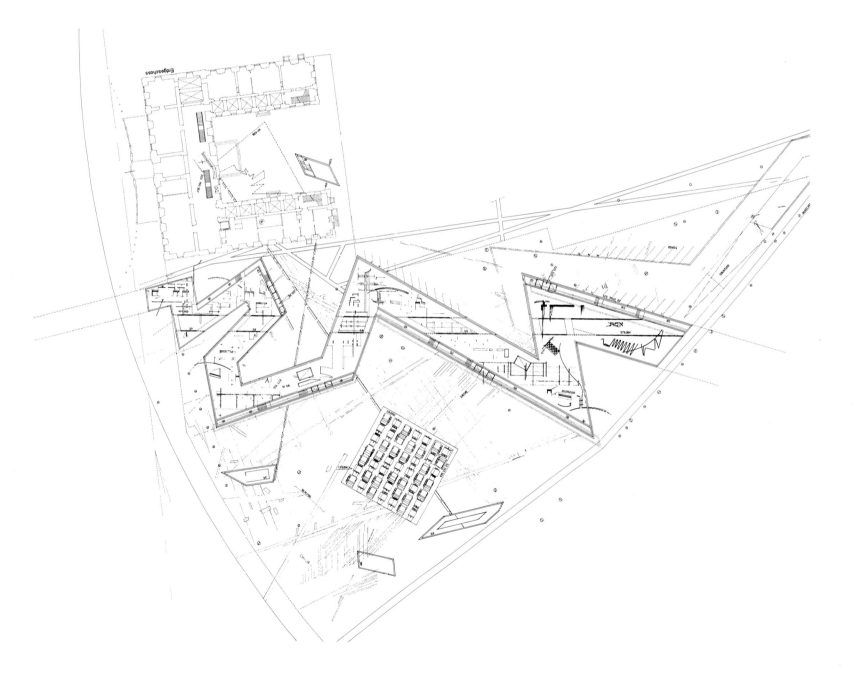

ABOVE: MODEL, INNER STRUCTURE OF BUILDING; *BELOW*: GROUND FLOOR PLAN

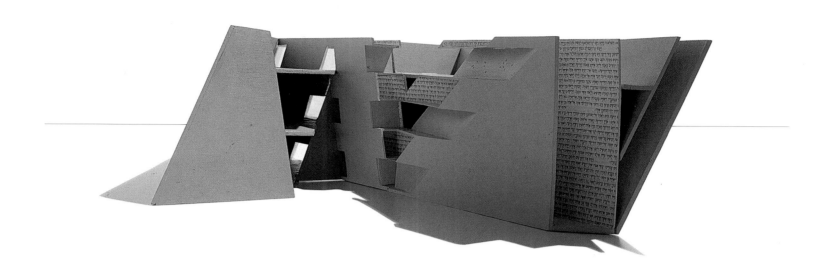

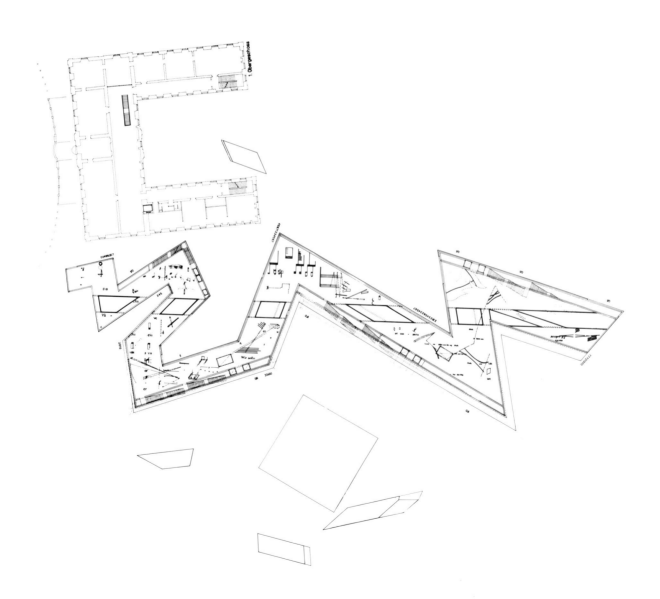

ABOVE: MODEL, INNER STRUCTURE OF THE BUILDING; *BELOW*: FIRST FLOOR PLAN

ABOVE: MODEL, INNER STRUCTURE OF THE BUILDING; *BELOW*: SECOND FLOOR PLAN

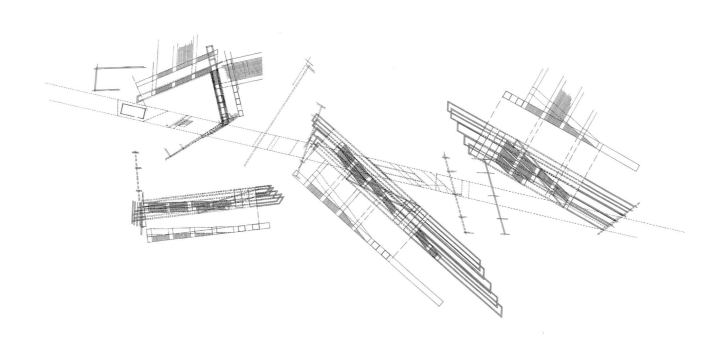

ABOVE: MODEL, VIEW FROM THE EAST; *BELOW*: PLANS AND ELEVATIONS OF THE STAIRS

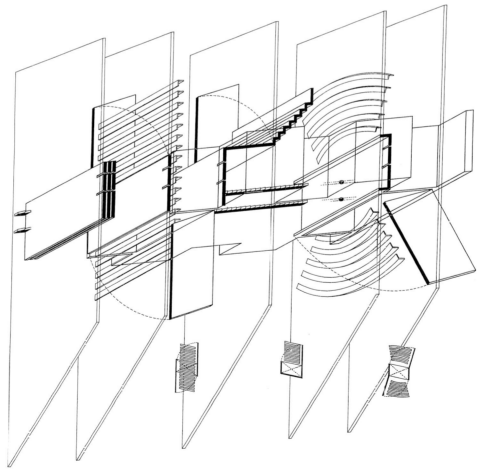

ABOVE: MODEL, VIEW FROM THE EAST; *BELOW*: THEATRE OF THE VOID

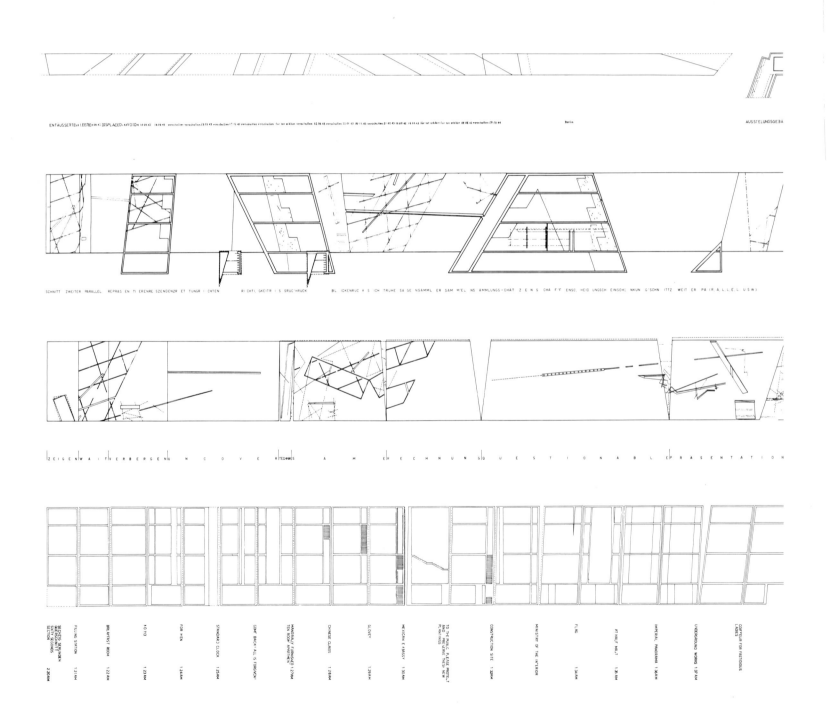

ABOVE L TO R: MODEL, VIEW FROM THE EAST, VIEW FROM LINDENSTRASSE; *BELOW:* SECTIONS AND ELEVATIONS

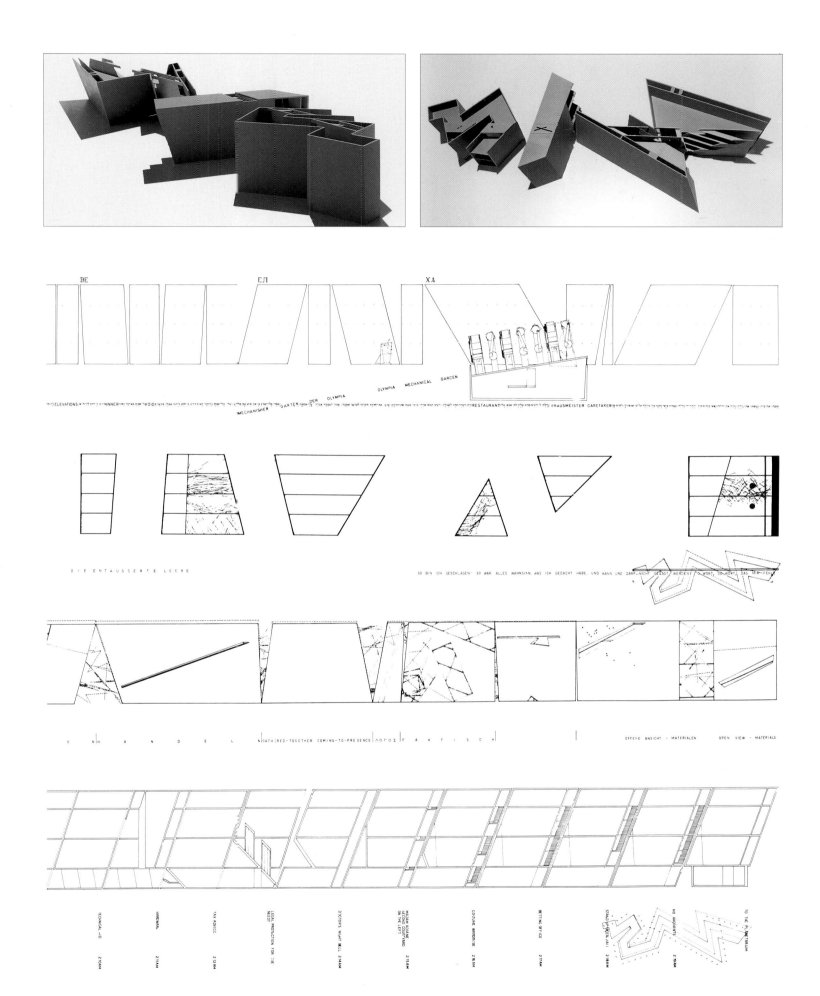

ABOVE L TO R: MODEL, INNER STRUCTURE; *BELOW*: SECTIONS AND ELEVATIONS

LEBBEUS WOODS, EAST AND WEST BERLIN, CAPTIVE CITIES

BERLIN / PARIS
MONUMENTS OR MODELS OF THOUGHT

ALSOP & LYALL, BERLIN BERLIN, THE CITY THERMOMETER

Kristin Feireiss, gallery owner and exhibition organiser, managed to persuade several architects from all over the world to contribute their ideas and architectural visions for Berlin and following this success she launched another project to deal with the urban future of Paris. The drawings, illustrations and texts are the subjects of exhibitions in both cities and of extensive publications.

Theoretically, an exhibition of architectural visions could not take place these days, as dreams don't seem to exist any more. Previously, the situation was different. We only have to remember the Glaserne Kette (Glass Chain) and Archigram, the most extreme antagonists one could imagine. Whilst the Glass Chain was the epitome of visionary architecture in Germany at the start of the century, and considered architecture to be the 'Realm of messianic expectations' setting the myth of the organic world over technology and the city, Archigram in London at the start of the 60s, glorified technology and spoke of 'the sparkling game of the machine and technical services'. In spite of their contrasting stances, these two tendencies acted always according to Bruno Taut's call 'Be Utopian!' What is relevant to the situation today? Is this call still heard, or more importantly followed? Or do the waters which Taut called the parting line between Utopia and construction flow again in the sense of what is accessible, workable? Is there still a body of concepts which consider urban space as a political aesthetic category? Dieter Hofman Axtheim gives them no chance today. According to him, the thirst for experience and experimentation at the end of the 60s does not exist anymore. Is this then the reality? Even though I was very tempted to grant that he was right, the building up of the exhibition confronted me with experiences which were palpably different.

My concept, which I outlined to the selected participants, held to the thesis that Berlin, from the start of the 20th century, has contributed to the development of the urban plan. The decadence of the 20th century is illustrated in an exemplary manner in Berlin. The guidelines for the participants specify 'We are looking for an outstanding development for the future, resulting from cultural, urban, geographic and political situations of Berlin – and that of the two parts of the city.

It is not a question of an architectural Utopia stemming from an overflowing and proliferating imagination, but of projects which carry with them the seeds of their realisation. Even if such projects, completely stretched from reality, could be justified in an era when only mass construction counted. What is important today is to present architectural concepts which mix both vision and necessity. The participants had to choose a place in the heart of the city which they judged to be significant for the development of conceptual alternatives.

In making the selection we have to take into account pragmatic points of view and extensive knowledge of the aesthetic level. But equally we should provide the young generation with a chance for expression; they will contribute their work to the world of tomorrow and replace their lesser practical experience by a creativeness without preconceptions. A passionate dialogue could occur – that is my hope.   *Kristin Feireiss*

CEDRIC PRICE, THE CITY ANALOGUE

COOP HIMMELBLAU, THE DISPLACING OF OUR BODIES INTO THE TOWN

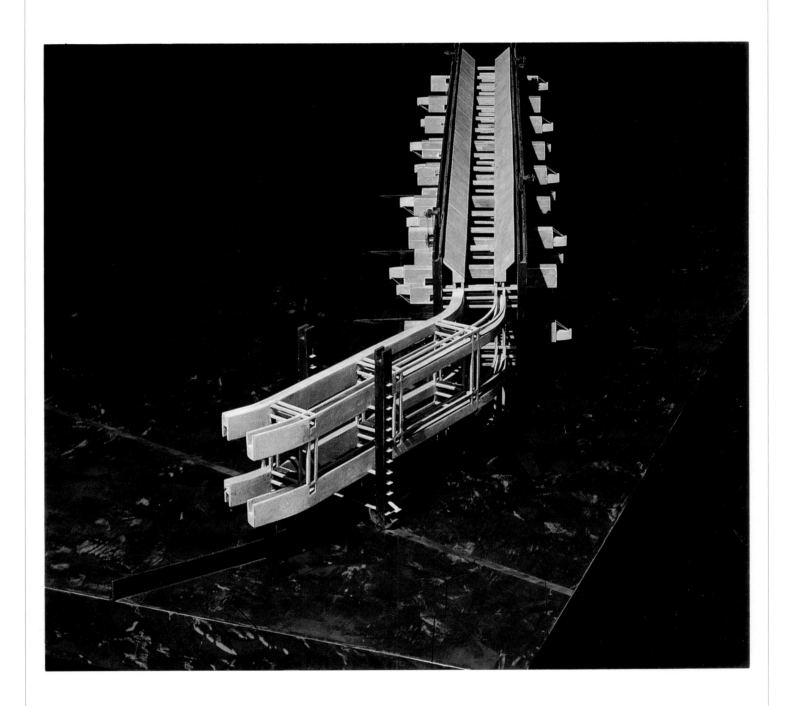

Morphosis, Berlin Wall – Line and Volume. The Berlin Wall divides this historic city into two halves, making an arbitrary edge between 'Western World' and 'Soviet Block', separating diverse political and economic philosophies. Whether the partition is seen as temporary or as permanent, the wall has ultimately left a lasting impression on the city. The project is scaled to reflect its edge condition and its location adjacent to the Brandenburg Gate, and it's conceived as an object structure stitching together the Tiergarten and the DMZ emptiness. Our intention is to create a permanent, living monument which will concretise and reconnect the fissure which is the Berlin Wall

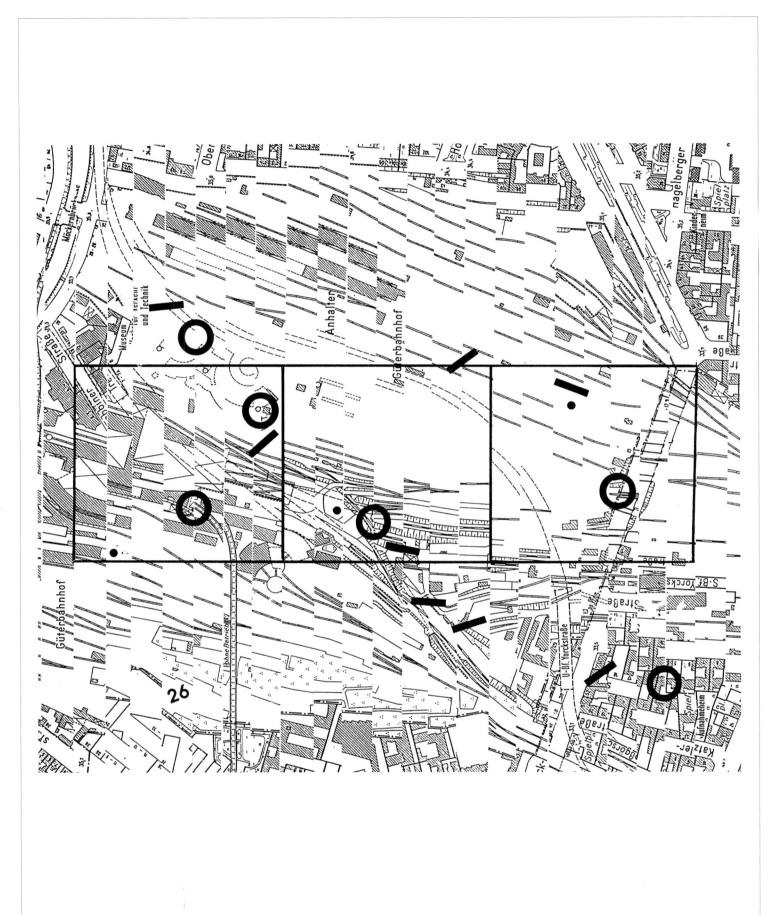

Bernard Tschumi, Asphalte. The Fun Fair. It is the first functional film set (the forms here have no architectural existence and were only created by the movements of actors and objects) Each of these elements is going to play a determining role in the scene. The platform will render more moving the fall of the acrobat, the hung cloth is made to receive the Chinese shadows, the swing for swinging, full or empty, the huge canvas at the back of the tent, for being agitated and torn by the wind. In a brief moment, several facades and gables appear.

ABOVE: MARK MACK, A TOWN OF LITTLE GARDENS AND AN AGGLOMERATION OF FISHERMEN; *BELOW*: ELISABETH & GOTTFRIED BOHM, A BACK BONE FOR GITSCHINER STRASSE

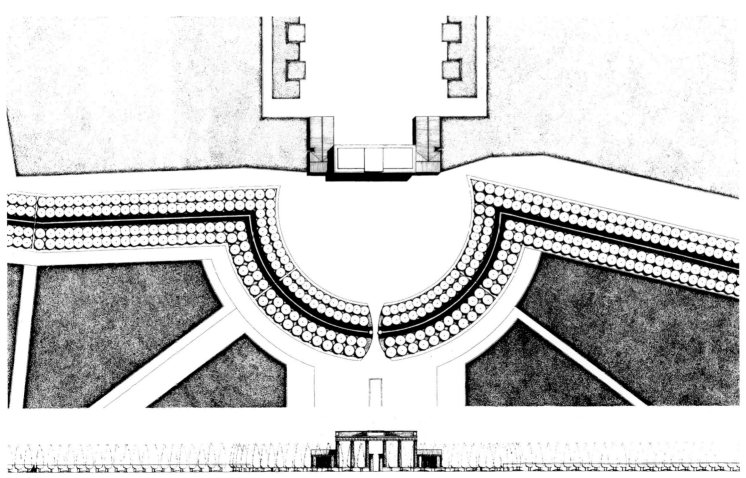

ABOVE: ARCHITECTURE-STUDIO, A NETWORK OVER THE WALL; *BELOW*: STANLEY TIGERMAN, BERLIN 2000

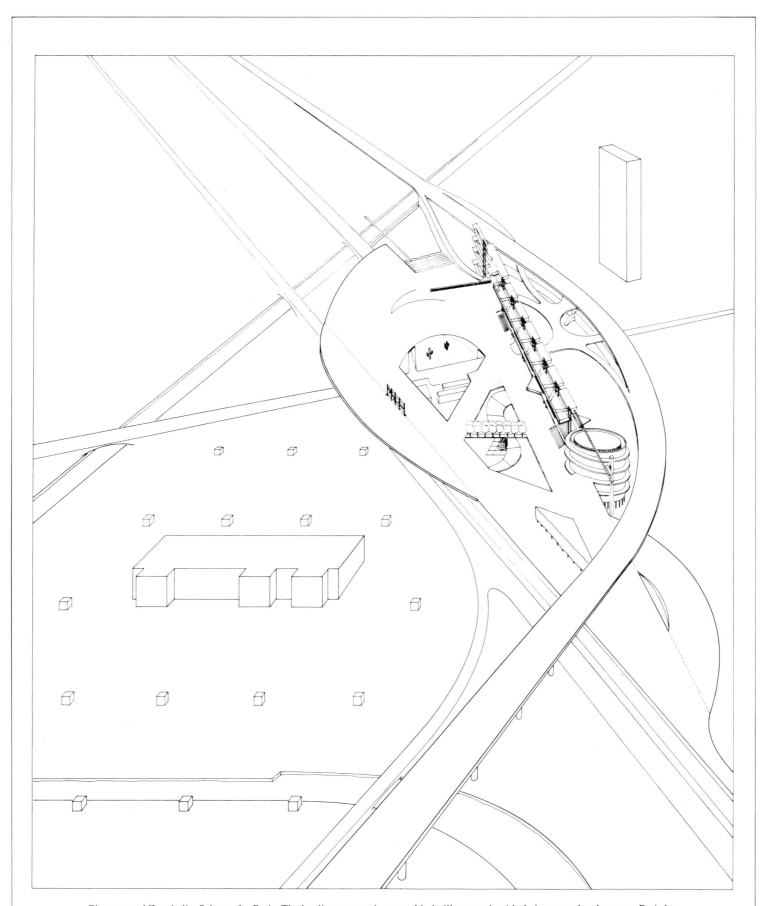

Gigantes and Zenghelis, Scheme for Paris. The banlieux are no longer orbital villages and, with their recent development, Paris has effectively urbanised its colonies. The resulting pressure on the centre can ease only with a transfer of facilities outwards which suggests that the zone between the périphérique and the petite ceinture transforms from 'wall' to an activated circular resource. The zone already has its own subculture. At present, apart from connecting the two bois, it is a latent fractured *magnito gorsk* of large-scale 19th- and 20th- century institutions and facilities. But for its inherent qualities to be realised, the zone needs to be continuous. The zone has the potential to be a contemporary equivalent to Paxton's Ring; a continuously unfolding landscape of events.

DANIEL KARPINSKI, THE CATHEDRAL OF THE REVOLUTION

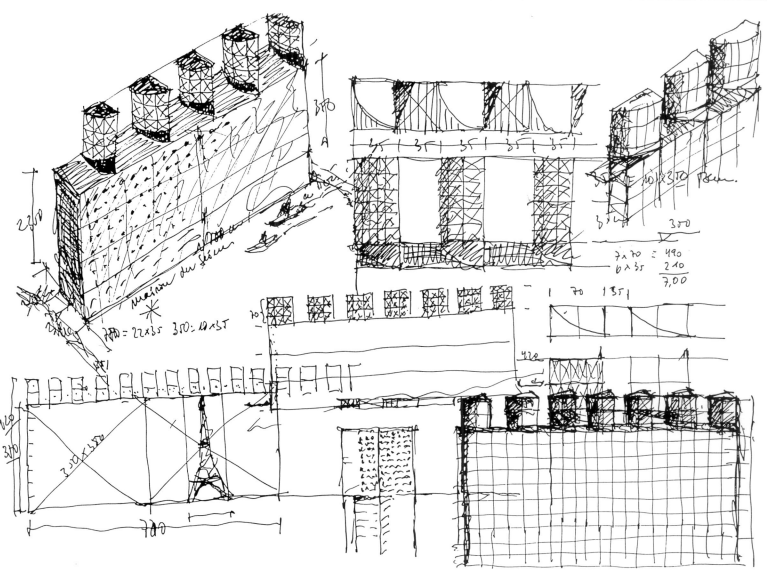

ABOVE: REIDERMEISTER, PHOTOMONTAGE OF PARIS SCHEME; *BELOW L TO R*

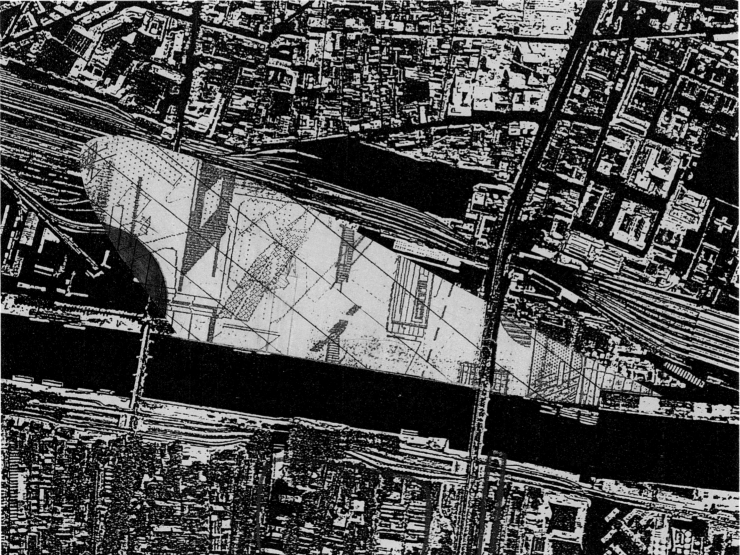

J P KLEIHUES, SKETCHES OF PARIS SCHEME; PETER WILSON, BETWEEN TWO SPEEDS

CLAUDIO SILVESTRIN
A SENSIBILITY OF SPACE

VICTORIAN HOUSE, INTERIOR TRANSFORMATION, HAMPSTEAD, LONDON, 1989, BLEACHED JAPANESE OAK STRIP FLOORING, CONCEALED STAIRS
SHOWING 10MM SHADOW GAP, SATIN GLASS FLOORLIGHTS, *L TO R*: FIRST-FLOOR DRESSING-ROOM; GROUND-FLOOR ENTRANCE

Strongly influenced by philosophy and art (most significantly the spatial concepts of Lucio Fontana and the sculpture of Richard Serra), in addition to the architecture of Mies van der Rohe, Claudio Silvestrin, a young Milanese architect currently based in London, is challenging the boundaries of conventional terminology with his primary, geometric forms – abstract configurations rendered in pure, natural materials and conceived in terms of free space. By reducing and abstracting architecture to its essential elements, including the 'free-standing' white-plastered wall which manifests itself as an autonomous object by means of a continuous shadow gap, Silvestrin aims to challenge familiar perceptions, demanding a new way of seeing, 'a new sensibility' that provides an alternative to the 'consumer anxiety' of the 80s. Selecting terms such as 'sensuality' and 'spirituality' to describe his architecture, in which the play of light on natural materials, the symmetry and the ideal rendering of geometric forms establishes a continuity with classical principles, Silvestrin believes in creating an atmosphere of free, yet disciplined space, intensifying the emotions and discourse of the figures within.

Not surprisingly, he has found many of his clients among the dealers of the international art world, who perceive his architecture primarily in terms of minimal art, existing in equilibrium with the work of artists such as Donald Judd, Carl Andre and Alan Charlton in the galleries designed in London, Frankfurt and Florence. Other recent projects – a selection of which are presented here, together with extracts from his writings – include a Japanese restaurant, book dealer's offices, and patisserie in London and, most recently, a free-standing house in Majorca. In this work Silvestrin continues the tension, established in his urban designs, between the minimal space and purity of his architecture, and the chaos and chance of everyday reality, transforming it here into a dialogue between the organic, irrational beauty of nature and the abstract, logical reasoning of man.

In his reverence for nature, for simplicity and spirituality, and for reducing objects in order to perceive the essence of things – principles which will determine the realisation of future projects in New York and Los Angeles – Silvestrin seems to look towards the 21st century, towards a future which, while lacking the nostalgia of the late 20th century, will at the same time acknowledge its continuing allegiance to the past. *Clare Farrow*

ABOVE L TO R: CANELLE PATISSERIE, LONDON, 1988, FULL-TONE ACID-ETCHED 12MM GLASS FACADE WITH DISPLAY CUBE; RUNKEL-HUE-WILLIAMS GALLERY, LONDON, 1989, BLEACHED JAPANESE OAK STRIP FLOORING; *BELOW L AND R*: WAKABA JAPANESE RESTAURANT, LONDON, 1987, CURVED SATIN GLASS, WHITE OILED BEECH INTERIOR

Destroying clutter is seeing the 'thickness' of space, the depth of the world. My task is to render space as free space, that is to say to make its invisible thickness visible: not an object for manipulation, not a locus for clutter, nor something to conquer. Taking possession of space is precisely what is not wanted. The architectural work must open up space and preserve it. Unoccupied space is not useless or wasted or lacking. The emptiness in a jar, in a corner, in a lawn of a cloister is not nothing. On the contrary. The space in a wine glass is what makes the vitreous body a glass. Rendering visible the invisibility of space means seeing beyond the image-screen of our vision, it means to see metaphysically: to see beyond, to pierce for constructing a something not yet there. Here constructing is not intended only as producing, it's not only setting-up and erecting. This is what technological building design is. The essence of construction lies neither in piling up layers of building materials nor in ordering them according to a plan, but solely in the opening up: when we set up a new space another 'atmosphere' opens up precisely through what is set up. Thus the architectural work is a positing that constructs: that is, founds, erects and opens up a new seeing. This new seeing wants to be the envisionment of the perfect.CS

NEUENDORF PLACE, MAJORCA, 1990 (COMPLETION 1991), 1ST-FLOOR CORRIDOR LEADING TO MASTER BEDROOM, BATHROOM AND DRESSING-ROOM, PAINTED PLASTER WALLS
SHOWING CONTINUOUS 10MM SHADOW GAP, SANTANYI STONE FLOOR, 6M STONE BENCH

Walls make space irrespective of man. Man's self-assertive will wills the cluttering of such space. But the mute force which projects from a free wall 'is' space. Man then cleverly (or so he thinks) reduces such force by making walls mere supports for his objects, his possessions. In the principle of the courtyard, walls make a perfect (enclosed) space: when we enter it we feel in a place. The perfect configuration of few figures opens up the possibility to imagine the mass of air inhabiting the room that we call space. Each figure is enhanced by space and the few earthly materials reveal all their splendour. The earth is rendered by the purity of the material's surrounding properties – surface, colour, thickness and weight – and not by figurative nature-imitation ornaments. With the minimum number of objects, of materials, of figures, of lines, of colours, of signs, the invisibility of space almost vanishes: space is, at least intuitively, visible. With this minimum, we let space be present, space is no longer objectified, conquered. It is rather preserved as free space. It is grasped and held as 'thing' and no longer as object. It is the ontological sense of space that has to be understood. With this minimum we render our horizon with few and simple figures. With a visual and clear order of lines in equilibrium and in symmetry, one feels at peace. The ideal configuration of elegant simplicity renders a feeling of serenity, of tranquility. The simplest geometric figures, free from impurity, are the nearest to the idea of perfection: with the square and the circle, the cube and the sphere, with the straight line and the subtle curve, any form of struggle ceases, the cogito gives up doubting. When in a work these geometric forms are in-

NEUENDORF PLACE, 1990, *L*: ABSTRACT PLAN SHOWING 110M STONE PATH AND FREE-STANDING WALL, 600M² VILLA RENDERED IN LOCAL RED-BROWN SOIL PIGMENT, 3.5X40M ELEVATED SWIMMING-POOL; *ABOVE R*: 12X12X9M COURTYARD CUBE WITH 0.83MX9M ENTRANCE, SANTANYI UNPOLISHED STONE, SOIL RENDERING; *BELOW R*: DINING AREA

dependent from metaphysical, theological or anthropological representation, they assert themselves, thus avoiding the speculative claims associated with personal authorship. When a form is not referential, when it is not delivering our nostalgic mnemonic images, in other words when it is not negated by one's own self-assertive will, the geometric form appears ambiguous, indeterminable, a non-entity, suggesting a multitude of readings, a possibility for other possibilities, a possibility for a new sensibility. The ideal configuration frees one's vision from the fashionable objects which resemble finitude, thus the feeling of durable calm. The body of the ideal figures, being of those earthly materials which 'are' solidity, immobility, peacefulness, render a configuration like that of Rafaello's portraits in which flesh is rendered to resemble clay, plaster, stone. Thus the feeling of durability, endurance. A vision of a world of figures immobilised in stillness: time is arrested, time is suspended, figures in the absoluteness of their presence, without a future or a past, in fatality. A vision of a place impregnated with grand calm, powerful, strong, awesome. The envisionment of the perfect demands a close understanding of the life elements and of the site materials; this is by far a superior criteria than that of novelty. The manipulation of materials, crafted with constancy towards perfection, transforms the material. The stone, dematerialised, loses its hardness. The wall, invisibly suspended, wins over gravity. The sun, pierced through deep and tiny openings, loses its over-glaring heat and is enhanced to its magnificence. The ideal manipulation transforms the site and yet the site is not disintegrated.CS

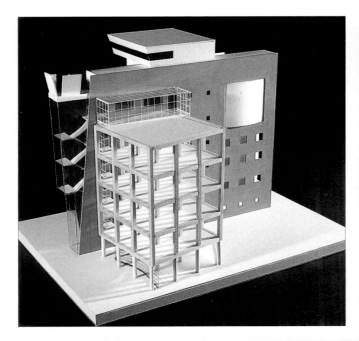

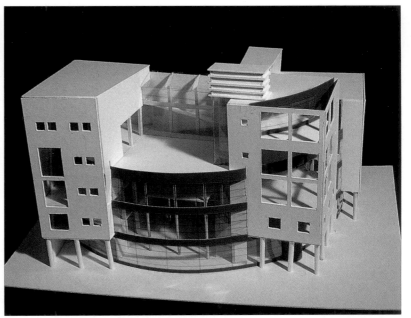

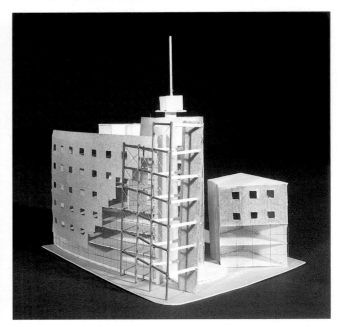

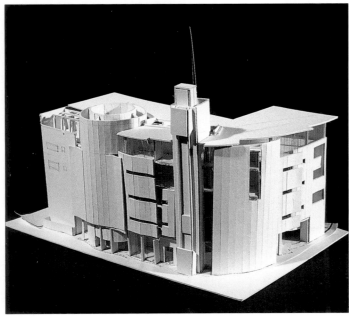

MODELS OF THE SCHEMES *ABOVE L* TO *R*: GOODENOUGH, ANWEN HUGHES; *CENTRE L* TO *R*: UNDERWOOD, GRIFFITHS; *BELOW L* TO *R*: HAHN, WONG

CATHERINE COOKE AND IVOR RICHARDS

ARGUMENTS AND FACTS
Fifth Year work at the University of Wales

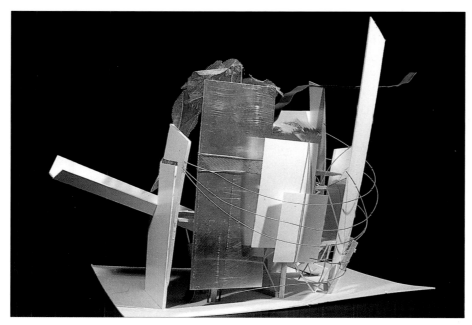

PEASE, MODEL OF SCHEME

With leading schools worldwide bringing theoreticians into the studio, Catherine Cooke's recent collaboration with Ivor Richards at the Welsh School of Architecture shows how stimulating the invitation to produce a narrative architecture can be when the brief is rich.

The final year project in architecture school ought to be one of life's great creative opportunities. Well equipped with the technical knowledge for big buildings that is reinforced, as in most countries, by a year in practice, it is the last chance most young architects will have for years to show what they can do if left alone with a large problem.

In Britain, the demise of truly open competitions – indeed, after recent notorious 'interventions', the dearth of all competitions – has eliminated that traditional vehicle for stretching youthful abilities and advancing architectal speculation. In Cardiff, many of the forty-strong fifth year are taking international competition briefs as the subject of their major final project. Some are tackling the Acropolis Museum project, determined to get schemes in for the competition before reworking them into diploma projects. Others are tackling the recent Bibliotheque National competition brief. In the University of Wales' course structure, however, these students have just returned from their year out in offices, with all the inhibitions to bold speculation and loss of confidence in large-scale design which that otherwise vital experience can produce. Invited as a Visiting Fellow for the year by the Head of School, Professor Richard Silverman, and Design Professor Ivor Richards, my first task was to help set them a three-week hors d'oeuvre that would stimulate the taste-buds for architecture again after year-long diets of building.

As a problem we sought something closely related to the real world of affairs which they have left – and as the project progressed, that became more true than we could have expected in this case. As an architectural task, it was intended to offer the potential for development of a rich architectural narrative.

Before Eastern Europe started such dramatic upheavals, the spotlight of world attention and speculation was focused on the process of reconstruction under way in the Soviet Union. At the centre of this perestroika process is a unique newspaper called called *Argumenty i Fakty – Arguments and Facts*. Like the other leading organ of glasnost, Ogonek, it is old-established and entirely officially produced, but under particularly courageous and intelligent editorship it has become the sharpest cutting edge of democratisation and the world's largest selling newspaper. At five kopeks, its weekly readership is now estimated to be an extraordinary thirty million people. Of modest format, it concentrates on pithy presentation of facts and issues, and operates in an unprecedented way as a dialogue between individual citizens and officialdom. Questions sent in by readers – often very probing ones – are fearlessly posed to politicians, bureaucrats or whoever is appropriate, in a way that would have been unthinkable in the Soviet Union a few years ago. Where necessary, the editors persist till they get frank and factual replies, or till the arguments on an issue have been honestly presented. The paper was about to have a Western collaborator, *Arguments & Facts International*. This results from the initiative of a small group of British journalists and academics whose aim is to extend that dialogue about the reality of today's Soviet Union into the international arena, as an information base for Western professions, industry and general public.

The brief we set was for the Western headquarters of *Arguments & Facts International*. The client, as the brief described it, was 'a small editorial team of highly motivated and imaginative people' who 'know that the communications vehicle they are creating is potentially a major catalyst of change and interaction, and of far greater power than a normal newspaper or magazine. The building is therefore to be something which itself serves as a catalyst to contact and dialogue.'

The editorial accommodation was small: other appropriate activities and use of the rest of the site were for the designers to conceive. The task was to create an architecture that communicates; that actively catalyses cultural consciousness and provokes the public mind to engage with the cultural reality of this extraordinary historical situation of the late eighties. Introductory lectures and an extensive bibliography (typically not read till later!) demanded that they engage with the multiple architectural implications of 'communications' in today's cultural space.

Thus the architectural task for the building was framed around three parameters. The design must have some narrative content larger than the mere fulfillment of function. As a form, the building must make a coherent statement about its spatial organisation and its tectonic structure. It must address its context in London and on the global arena.

Architecturally it had thus to balance a complex cultural ambiguity: to whom would the building 'belong', and in whose language was it to be read? If British architecture is dogged by an increasing mistrust of cultural modernisation, Soviet architecture is as yet directionless, struggling even to re-establish its existence above the lumbering mammoth of the Soviet construction industry that has nearly annihilated it. In defining a new language for the new polity, it faces the dilemma of the whole country: how to handle a reality that is materially bankrupt and primitive when the image it would like to maintain is one of sophistication and world power status?

The site for the building is a prominent corner of London's Fleet Street, where only a few architectural moments of the thirties now remain – classicised art deco for the conservative *Daily Telegraph* and dynamically slick for the popular *Daily Express* – either as ghosts of its former role as a hub of world press communications or to echo such archetypal newspaper buildings of Modernism as Loos's *Chicago Tribune* or the Vesnins' *Leningrad Pravda*.

Besides having two prominent elevations, the site is split at street level by the pedestrian right-of-way into a typical old yard of the old city. Some designs used that to create a separate and less public realm for the journal's offices; others saw these functions as programmatically the open, accessible motor of the public activity of debate, exhibition, business and cultural contact-making, in the often-dramatic spaces created on the rest of the site. One project reflected the growing political tensions and pluralism of the USSR by providing each individual Soviet republic with a voice to speak from its individual accomodation; most envisaged the building's facilities as a unified territory available to all serious interest groups democratically. Many projects used the full gamut of Western electronic technologies to effect the mutual learning process they envisaged, and a building technology redolent of the space age. Others took an opposite view, using simple, Soviet-level building techniques to create spatial pleasures and diversity that would catalyse direct person-to-person encounters between the Western public and Soviet guests. Most provided college-like accommodation for a number of such guests to be staying on site.

In constructing a formal narrative, transparency and physical openness provided natural and direct symbols for *glasnost*, as well as practical means for maximising public involvement in the building. Some projects very explicitly played glass against solid and impenetrable surfaces; others juxtaposed symbolic and formal expressions of the dynamism and unpredictability of debate against solid frameworks of 'the old'. Some made explicit references to the stylistic languages of Soviet architecture, grappling in different ways with the conflicting associations which Avant-Garde Modernism has aquired in West and East, or the confused readings which the Western Post-Modern eye can make of Stalinist 'classicism'.

As the three-week project proceeded, *Argumenty i Fakty's* editor, Vladislav Starkov, became the subject of almost daily reports in Western newspapers, after public criticism by President Gorbachev of certain items in the paper, and three successive demands for his resignation from the Communist Party Central Committee. But they are not his employers and have no power to force his departure. As I write, it is reported that leading staff of Soviet television have vowed to strike in solidarity with the *Argumenty i Fakty* journalists unless the demands are withdrawn.

Such news bulletins may have helped the students to keep drawing through the night: I never asked them. The pressure was intentionally very tight. This was a three-week project, with two stiff interim juries before a ten-day period for final design and presentation. In the maturity and sophistication achieved, and in the richness of organisational and architectural concepts developed into detailed building proposals in three weeks work, the project exceeded even optimistic pedagogical expectations. More important, almost all the forty-odd students had exceeded their own estimation of their personal capabilities, and spontaneously admitted to a new level of engagement with the forthcoming major project as an investigation of current architectural issues.

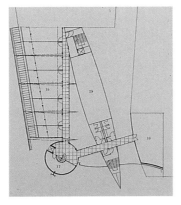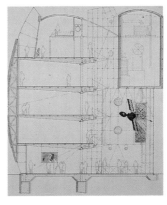

WARD, PLAN AND SECTION